THIS PATH I TOOK

THIS PATH I TOOK

Gerald Ribeiro

Edited by Robert French

iUniverse, Inc.
New York Lincoln Shanghai

THIS PATH I TOOK

iUniverse books may be ordered through booksellers or by contacting:

iUniverse
2021 Pine Lake Road, Suite 100
Lincoln, NE 68512
www.iuniverse.com
1-800-Authors (1-800-288-4677)

ISBN-13: 978-0-595-37824-1 (pbk)
ISBN-13: 978-0-595-82199-0 (ebk)
ISBN-10: 0-595-37824-2 (pbk)
ISBN-10: 0-595-82199-5 (ebk)

Printed in the United States of America

Contents

Foreword by Robert French ix

Preface xiii

CHAPTER 1   Dimming of the Light 1

CHAPTER 2   Menace Because of Society 7

CHAPTER 3   Alternative Sentencing 11

CHAPTER 4   Liberated Territory 17

CHAPTER 5   The End Doesn't Justify the Means 21

CHAPTER 6   Legend 25

CHAPTER 7   Superfly Syndrome 30

CHAPTER 8   Behind the Walls: Prince of the City 36

CHAPTER 9   G's Machine 42

CHAPTER 10   Living Dead 45

CHAPTER 11   Hitting Bottom 51

CHAPTER 12   Trying to Get Recovery 56

CHAPTER 13   Getting to the Here and Now 60

CHAPTER 14   Rebirth 67

CHAPTER 15   Power Shared 71

CHAPTER 16   Yes or No 75

CHAPTER 17   Stayin' Alive 79

CHAPTER 18   About Political Capital and Me 83

CHAPTER 19   Teach the Children 85

CHAPTER 20   What Has Love Got to Do with It? 91

CHAPTER 21   Empathy Disorder 93

CHAPTER 22   Facing the Reality of My Mortality 97

CHAPTER 23   This Path I Took 103

Notes. 109

Acknowledgments

The following people read and thoughtfully commented on drafts of this work: Dan Bellm, Phillip Beauregard, Manuela Da Costa, Patty Hnatiuk, Maryel Locke, Laurence Locke, and Maria Rosario. Each made suggestions that improved the book.

Professor Jama Lazerow (Wheelock College), whose extensive research on the Black Panther party in Boston and New Bedford includes two interviews with Gerald, made sure that the chapters covering the early 1970s accord with the historical record.

Helen Salgado's careful transcription of the taped interviews and initial stab at organizing the far-ranging material were invaluable in the process of making the material become a book.

Shelly Perry, with whom Gerald shared his last years, deserves thanks not only for her insight in the final editing of the book after his death, but also for its very existence. Together they created a "clean, well-lighted place" in which he could tell his story.

Finally, I am deeply grateful to Gerald for asking me to help him write his story. I look back on our agreement to embark on this project as a grain of sand around which a pearl of friendship formed.

R.F.

Foreword

We had lost hope, and we needed a story to understand what had happened to us.

—*Julia Alvarez, In the Time of Butterflies*[1]

Gerald Ribeiro's life bears out the observation "Extreme hopes are born of extreme misery."[2] Born and bred in New Bedford, Massachusetts, Gerald reflected about his past, "you can't get any more underclass than being of color, poor, homeless, addicted, living with a terminal disease." In 1989, early in his recovery, he co-founded New Bedford Treatment on Demand, a grassroots response to the "twin epidemics" of substance abuse and AIDS—so characterized because of the rapid spread of HIV infection among injection drug users who, like Gerald, contracted the virus by sharing blood-contaminated needles.

Initially a call for more drug treatment, Treatment on Demand enlarged its field of view to include the underlying causes of AIDS and drug abuse: poverty and oppression that extinguish hope for a better life. In neighborhoods and cultural communities most devastated by the confluence of drug addiction and AIDS, recovery is not only a process of personal change, but also people's concerted efforts on economic, social, and political fronts to improve their lives. The book *Dying for Growth: Global Inequality and the Health of the Poor*[3] includes Treatment on Demand on its worldwide list of 62 organizations highlighted for their work for social and economic justice.

When I joined the Board of Directors of Treatment on Demand in 1992, Gerald and I teamed up writing grant proposals. A friend, I readily agreed to help him record his life story. A social anthropologist by training, I welcomed the chance to examine how culture, color, and class shaped his world, bounded his choices, and became a lens for self-realization and political understanding.

This book is a distillation of interviews conducted in Gerald's home over the course of more than five years. They were often abbreviated or postponed because of Treatment on Demand deadlines as well as the exigencies of my job running an underfunded, community-based agency serving low-income children and families. Chronicling the past repeatedly took a backseat to keeping up with today.

Memories are like sandbars, continually reworked and reshaped over time by the currents of subsequent experience, present circumstance, and evolving perspective. The passage of time allowed us to do some retakes of events and people. It also tempered the story, revealing some victories to be illusory or short-lived, like getting my partner into a treatment program that she soon left. Gerald became a proud grandfather, he got married, his disease progressed, Treatment on Demand celebrated its tenth anniversary. In the hospital up to his death on December 22, 2002, Gerald talked about expanding on some sections in his narrative. While considering this account of his life (as well as his lived life) to be a work in progress, he left no doubt about wanting to publish it.

Though self-effacing about the limits of his formal education and the reach of his vocabulary, Gerald was a powerful, eloquent speaker who drew from the wellspring of African American oratorical traditions. Using the interview transcripts prepared by Helen Salgado, I pared down, spliced, melded, sequenced, and chaptered the material. Gerald had the final say; the book has seen only minor editing since he last reviewed it. Punctuation generally follows the pattern of his narration. For reasons apparent in the narrative, some names have been changed.

As autobiographer, Gerald served as gatekeeper. Some details of his life had been lost to pain; others were too painful to tell. To dwell on what is missing is to miss the point of his narrative; he did not intend for it to be about him alone, but to make the lived experience of addicts, people with HIV, and other stereotyped, marginalized people accessible and real. As James Olney maintains in his book *Metaphors of Self*, "autobiography is more universal than it is local, more timeless than historic, and more poetic in its significance than merely personal." Accordingly, we can learn from autobiography, as from poetry and other literature, about "what forms have proved possible in humanity" as we tackle the paramount question "How shall I live?"[4] Responding to the pervasive predisposition to write off people like him as somehow less than human, Gerald's story serves as a compelling, impassioned case that his life and the lives of others like him can provide us with insight into the inclusive human experience.

In our interviews, Gerald reflected on the meaning and course of his life from different vantage points, for no one perspective will engender a full accounting of ourselves. He contemplated how poverty and discrimination stamped his life and blocked pathways of opportunity, while conceding self-responsibility for choices he had made along the way. Recognizing that he was a casualty in the United States government's War on Drugs (a "war" largely waged against poor communities of color), he considered how his experience as an addict and living with the virus contributed to his personal and political development. He unflinchingly examined the dissonant motives that drove his efforts to get active addicts into treatment. The different perspectives, or "voices," in his personal narrative resemble the progression in a jazz song in which different players take the lead for a time, while the others play behind them.

Gerald received numerous awards for his work and for the organization he founded. He had the ear of a host of local and state officials, carried weight with the media, and was a sought-after speaker. While he won public recognition in his community and across the state as a drug treatment advocate and AIDS activist, he chafed at such labels as being fixed and limiting. "No one today is purely *one* thing," notes Edward Said, "Labels…are no more than starting-points, which if followed into actual experience for one moment are quickly left behind."[5] Gerald was always improvising, guided by a faith that the dissonance in his life that came with improvisation would arrive at a resolution as it does in the improvised jazz songs of John Coltrane, Miles Davis, and other musicians he admired.

For Gerald, self-understanding and establishing his connection with humankind were inextricably intertwined. Gerald's expanding consciousness of the human community was like the widening ripples when a stone breaks the surface of a pond. When he said about active addicts, "I know the bottom line is that I am no different than any of the people that are still out there in terms of what's inside of me," he expressed his deep-felt belief in the commonality, the value, and the potential of all people. In his time, he was an advocate for addicts, for people living with the virus, for African Americans, for poor people, and ultimately for all people who face oppression in any shape or form. As he put it, his struggle affirmed the dignity, humanity, and rights of all people. In this spirit, Gerald extended the concept of recovery beyond the process of overcoming drug addiction to encompass healing from all kinds of oppression. The quality and compass of Gerald's love, generosity, and sensibility find expression in the writing of Paulo Freire: "As the oppressed, fighting to be human, take away the oppressors' power to dominate and suppress, they restore to the oppressors the humanity they had lost in the exercise of oppression."[6] Gerald's and my dissimilar life circumstances did not so much pose barriers as present opportunities to learn from one another.

Gerald's community-building work recognized and sustained the interplay of individual growth and social change. "Community is like the layers of an onion," he liked to say Community is global, embracing all living things, and at the same time, it is immediate, concrete, embodied in his day-to-day life in which he acknowledged the uniqueness, worth, strengths, and needs of each person. It is in this spirit of community that Gerald gives this book to you.

Robert French, Ph.D.
New Bedford, Massachusetts

Preface

People like to define me as a drug treatment advocate and AIDS activist. That is not what I am. Those are some of the issues that I have to deal with in my personal life, in the community where I live, and within the broad context of what's going on in this world. My story is not just about addiction or the fact that I'm able to live with a terminal illness and remain positive about my life and my future. Those are just symptoms of the deeper issue of how outside forces got in the way of my relationships with my fellow men and women, where oppression created a self-fulfilling prophecy, where feeling like I was less than, as a child, I acted out through my drug use.

I hope that my story will be helpful for people who have experienced oppression not just as it relates to substance abuse and AIDS and color, but other forms of oppression as well. Everybody has a story. My story is significant only in that it offers some clear examples that could help people understand what's going on in their own lives—to see that what they are experiencing is something that they are not alone with, first of all, and that there is a way of dealing with those issues head on.

I would like this book to help people to see that they can overcome barriers, learn from what they call *negative experiences*, redefine themselves, and take action to recover their life. They don't have to feel that the particular situation they're in that that's their story. Their story, like my story, can be one of transition and enlightenment—a story that says that life is not a destination, that you're always on a journey as long as you're breathing. As long as you're alive, you have the ability to learn and to continue to grow, to connect with other human beings and everything else on earth, to bring about changes that not only affect your life, but the community around you and even the global community.

I hope that this book will help people understand that when they hear the word *addict*, to know that an addict is not born, that there are conditions and circumstances that put people in so much pain that they resort to self-medication. This book is intended to personalize the whole issue of oppression, not only about being an addict, but about being Black, homeless, someone with the virus, someone with a limited education, someone with a lot of pain, someone who did at one time commit crime—what were the roots behind that? My story is about the negative side of an economic system and its effect on human beings, both the people who are oppressed because of that system and those that have lost their humanity because of their acts of oppression. It separates us as people, and I want this book to convey how that happens in little ways and in profound ways.

I hope that this book not only opens people's eyes, but also opens their hearts and motivates them to do something about all the inhumanity that happens. Seeing the other side of the street and having empathy are important, but action is even more important. I wanted to tell my story not just to illustrate social ills, but also to show that people can change their lives and their community.

I am coming from the lowest of the low, and my mission and who I'm about and what I'm aiming for come from that place. There's only one way for me to go, and that's up. That's what my intent is, it's part of every meeting, every conversation.

When I realize that there are countless people out there who have a similar vision for their life and for humanity, then my work for social change doesn't seem so overwhelming. I do my part and somebody else does their part, and somebody else does theirs, then the trickle becomes a river. I hope that this book can become a part of the greater work that people do in different ways, on different issues, using different channels of communicating, that can bring about that vision of a just society—a society where we can treat one another with respect, with equality, and contribute to a society that gives back to us.

Finally, I want to put my story down on paper for my own children, for them to be able to see what their father experienced—to have a record of my life, what I wanted to do, what I wanted to be, and the vision that I wanted to help create.

1

Dimming of the Light

Hawthorn Street where I delivered papers in the late fifties, early sixties was four or five blocks west of the Purchase Street neighborhood where I grew up. That short walk up the hill and I was in, what we used to call, the rich neighborhood. The people I saw were usually white and had a look of importance. The houses seemed massive and looked freshly painted. Wide, well-kept lawns. Big cars parked in big driveways. What impressed me were the broad spaces between the houses and the seemingly contented look on people's faces.

I would compare the spaciousness of the Hawthorn Street neighborhood to living down on Purchase Street, where tenement houses were so close to one another that if you took twenty steps from your house you would probably land in the next-door neighbor's living room. Backyards were mostly small and often blacktopped and front yards were almost non-existent. Instead of driveways and garages, cars parked in front of houses lining both sides of the street.

The house we lived in, 517 Purchase Street, was a three-decker tenement that is typical in New Bedford. It was located in the South Central area, where most Cape Verdean families of the city lived at that time. Our apartment was on the first floor and had three bedrooms. One bedroom was my parents'. My two sisters shared a bedroom, while the seven of us boys shared the third bedroom with its three beds. With all of us living in such a small space, we had to learn the art of compromise, patience, and concern for others. But lack of privacy was a source of frustration, and the solo walks up Hawthorn Street became a refuge for me.

I had two different feelings when I walked along Hawthorn Street. On one level, I would feel happy being in the peaceful setting with all that space. It was a time of escape from the reality I came from. Things looked so picture perfect up there. Part of me rationalized that the inequality between the two neighborhoods was natural; I accepted that because we were Cape Verdeans, we were supposed to be living in poor neighborhoods. But other times during my walks I felt sad, disappointed, that something was wrong with things being so different and unequal. There was no one I felt I could talk to about the thoughts running through my mind. So I kept them locked inside myself.

I was born in New Bedford, Massachusetts on December 30, 1951. My earliest memories are living in the Brickenwood projects. One day when I was four or five years old I saw my sister, who was eight or nine, changing my brother's diaper on the kitchen table. I came up behind her and scared her. When she turned around, the baby rolled off the table, landed on the floor, and screamed. When he died shortly after, I felt that it was my doing. Not so much before then, but definitely from that moment on I had a sad and lonely childhood, feeling like I was a bad person in a deep way.

Feeling I was responsible for my baby brother's death filtered how I saw myself not only as a child, but as a teenager, a young adult, all the way up to even now. I never completely absolved myself of that dirty deed. If someone could have seen how the circumstances of my baby brother's death had such an impact on me and could have explained it to me, I might have been able to see the incident for what it was. Because I didn't have that kind of support, I had to limp through life for many years and see myself as someone who had done the worst thing in my mind that you could do—besides taking your own life, to take somebody else's.

But helping a child to express himself was not a type of communication that happened in my family. That my mother and father had so many kids definitely didn't help things. Both my parents were first-generation Cape Verdean Americans, and having large families was still a part of their culture from the Cape Verde Islands. My father and his two brothers between them had over thirty kids. The more kids, the more hands, the more workers, the more ability to survive the harshness of the Cape Verdean land. That way of thinking that meant survival in their motherland wasn't necessary or even beneficial in this country.

Your mother and father play a major role in teaching you how to relate to people and how you see yourself in relationship to others. Though my mother had a stern side that she showed when she thought she needed to, she was very caring toward other people. Many people in the community called her "Mom." My father had an outgoing personality. Everywhere I went with him people knew and liked him and I wanted to be like that.

My father did construction and other jobs. Being Cape Verdean, he was the first to be laid off for the winter months and the last to be hired back in the spring. When he went down to city hall to get his veterans' benefits, the man would say, "Mr. Ribeiro, you're supposed to get fifty dollars, but I'm keeping ten." And he could do nothing about it.

Besides doing most of the childrearing, my mother sometimes worked in one of the many factories in the city. Between the two of them, we never starved, always had clothes on our back, and a roof over our heads. More than anything else, receiving government surplus food taught me that we were poor. We called it *Kennedy cheese, Kennedy peanut butter*, or *Kennedy* whatever food it was. While we never went without the basics, for a child to grow up healthy in all aspects, it is equally important to hear the words "I love you" as it is to have something to eat.

My father never, in my recollection, hugged me or told me that he loved me. Although my mother was nurturing, it was the same with her. Expressing love in an open, direct way was not part of our family culture. Many times my father said harsh things to me or about me like "He's a little sissy. Why don't I get you paper dolls to play with?" in reaction to me breaking my arm playing. When I lost or broke my glasses, he would say things like," I'm going to get you one of those straps that the secretaries wear so you will take better care of them." Where he was coming from was, "Damn, he breaks his arm, I gotta find money to pay for it." His response to my health problems only made me feel worse about myself.

When I got sick I got the most attention and nurturing from my mother. When I was real young, there was talk of the possibility of me having rheumatic heart fever. Then there was the broken arm. In the third grade, I had to have my appendix removed. Sometimes I used to fake being sick as a way of attracting the attention I craved from my mother and, risky as it was, my father.

Though I didn't get some of the things that I needed from my mother and father, they gave me plenty in terms of helping me understand on a real primal level that I am interconnected to others and that I am my brother's keeper. During the years I was an addict, my family never turned their back on me. My mother and father always worried about me and deeply cared about me.

The family unit wasn't just my parents and siblings. It reached beyond my immediate family to my cousins, aunts, and uncles. During the fifties and early sixties, before the hurricane dikes were built, the far South End of the city, where my cousins lived, used to get flooded when the hurricanes came. Because the house we lived in was the furthest north away from the water, sometimes my extended family would take shelter in our house, where we withstood the storm together, sharing food, water, laughter. When crisis happens, it's good to be able to depend on people and have people depend on you. That whole sense of belonging and feeling love, caring, and empathy toward others—all of those things that I believe in, that I stand for today, happened right within that house.

Church was a main part of our life growing up. I attended church regularly all the way up until I joined the army at age seventeen. I first attended Our Lady of Assumption, a Catholic church, and went as far as making my First Communion. During my grammar school years, my parents and family joined the Protestant church Reverend Manuel Chavier was starting down the South End. He was very compassionate, charismatic, and brought a more humanistic feeling to going to church.

At the five-year anniversary for my mother's death held at the church, Reverend Chavier talked about the importance of our family in building the church back in its early days, because between my father and his two brothers and their more than thirty kids, that was his Sunday school right there. He used to get the kids to go to the church and eventually the parents came. My father became head custodian of the church as a side job. We used to go to church on Tuesdays, Wednesdays, and three times on Sundays, because you went to Sunday school, then morning service, and the evening service.

Even though the church was primarily made up of Cape Verdeans, it was called the Portuguese Church of the Nazarene, because back then the Cape Verdeans saw themselves as being Portuguese. It was renamed the International Church of the Nazarene and now draws its congregation from the wider community. That the metal cross from my younger sister's funeral thirty-something years ago is right there on the pulpit in their new building shows how deeply entrenched our family was in the church.

Reverend Chavier's son and I became friends. I used to go over to his house in Fairhaven and we sang duets at the church. Reverend Chavier used to look at me and tell my mother and father, "That kid's going to be something one day, there's something about him." He was the first one that ever said that about me. No one else ever told me that coming up.

Reverend Chavier's impact on my life was like lighting a match in a dark room and how much light one flickering match brings to that room. He instilled in me the feeling that I could accomplish something. Through everything that I experienced, that light was burning in me.

I remember the first day of fourth grade at the T.A. Greene School like it was yesterday. You sat in whatever seat the teacher told you to sit in and then you'd stand up and say your name. When she came to me and I said my name, she said, "Ribeiro? Are you Bruce's brother?" I said yes. My brother Bruce was one grade ahead of me. She said, "Come up here." When I got up to her in front of the class, she put my back to the chalkboard, grabbed my face with her thumb and her forefinger, her thumbnail sticking into my chin, banged my head against the blackboard two times, *bam, bam*, and said, "That's to let you know who's boss in this class." People laughed and she told me to go sit down. I was totally embarrassed. She didn't do that to anybody else. Because they respected and, I think, were intimidated by the system, my parents' response was, "Well, you just make sure you don't do anything wrong."

Fifth grade was almost the same situation. Mrs. McMullen was so old that my father had her as a teacher. The first day of school she read me the riot act in front of everybody. Even though the school was in the heart of the Cape Verdean neighborhood, all of the school staff were white. I was taught to fear them from day one. I never had any real relationship with them.

My mother and father went only as far as sixth or seventh grade. They didn't see their children going on to be doctors, lawyers, or whatever our potential might be. As soon as my brothers turned sixteen and were old enough to quit school, they went to work. I was never pushed to do homework. There were never any major repercussions for getting a bad report card.

In the sixth grade, I scored near the top in the district on the achievement test. The school called my house. My parents got in touch with Reverend Chavier. Because people acted like what I had done was extraordinary, I suddenly felt special. In my school, only two other students scored as high as I did. Scoring the highest, Carlos L. was a light-skinned Cape Verdean with straight black hair—*light-skinned* meaning that you would think he was Portuguese. His family was middle class, where we were working class poor. Ricardo C. and I tied; he was another light-skinned Cape Verdean, but his hair was curlier than Carlos'. They were two golden boys, so to speak. I felt equal to them for a minute there.

After scoring so high on the achievement test, I began to feel better about myself. My childhood sadness lifted a little bit. That gave me the courage to try harder in school. I started to show interest in writing, wanting to put my thoughts down on paper.

I set my sights on becoming a veterinarian. I thought they were special because they could relate to animals. We always had animals at home—dogs, fish, turtles, parakeets. They always had a special part in my life. Animals give like unconditional love, where you don't have to prove yourself.

Toward the end of the sixth grade, you met with your guidance counselor to decide whether you were going to take *General Course, Business Course,* or *College Course. Business Course* was for people who wanted to work in the business field. *College Course* was for people who wanted to go on. *General* was for people who didn't plan on continuing their education after high school.

When I sat down with the guidance counselor and told him I wanted to take College Course, he said, "No, I don't think you should." I told him that I wanted to be a veterinarian. "You have to go to college for that, don't you?" He put me back in my place, basically telling me that my chances of going to college were slim to none and that I didn't need a college degree to work in a factory.

He was someone who I was taught to respect and to fear at the same time, and what he said must be true. But because of the big deal that had been made about my high scores on the achievement test, part of me believed I could do well. It was enough to carry me over in my struggle with the guidance counselor.

When I took the College Course in seventh grade, I wasn't prepared. I didn't have the fundamentals of reading, writing, and arithmetic. In the earlier grades, there was no one at home or in school to guide me along and assure me, "You can do it." Basically saying, "You can't do it, so just do this to get you by," they pushed me through one grade to the next.

2

Menace Because of Society

Growing up in the South End during my time, most Cape Verdeans were taught and believed that we were better than African Americans, the people whose fore-fathers were slaves. We called them *American colored people.* We saw ourselves as being brown, meaning that we didn't have the same privileges as the white popu-lation, but we weren't as bad off as the American colored people. There was a say-ing we used: "If you're white, you're all right; if you're brown, stick around; if you're Black, you're way back."

My brother-in-law Reggie is African American from Detroit. When my sister first started dating him, my mother and father made fun of him because he had distinct African features and a dark complexion. We bought into the idea that because we were of mixed ancestry, Portuguese and African, that we were better than him. Like other Cape Verdeans, I saw myself as being mostly Portuguese, a brown Portuguese person. It wasn't until my late teens that I learned that the Cape Verde Islands are off the west coast of Africa, not Portugal.

Cape Verdeans were supposed to be different because we came over here vol-untarily. *Voluntarily* misrepresents Cape Verdean migration, because Cape Verde was so poor and oppressed by hundreds of years of colonial misrule that people had to get away from there to find a better place to live. So whenever we talk about Blacks whose forefathers were slaves and whose families have been here for two, three hundred years and Cape Verdeans who came over because we wanted to, the difference isn't necessarily true. Cape Verdeans may have come over as crew on whaling ships or paid their way over and not have come over in shackles that you could visibly see, but the shackles that confined them are the same shackles that we deal with every day in this country right now: the shackles of the mind, the shackles of the spirit, the shackles of poverty and discrimination.

About halfway through seventh grade, my family moved up to the West End. This was in the early sixties, at a time when Cape Verdeans mainly lived in South Central and saw the West End as where the crazy, violent American colored people lived. I was worried that they were going to kick my ass. My first day at my new school, Keith Junior High, a Cape Verdean kid whose locker was next to mine, helped me open my locker. Ron and I quickly became good friends.

He was part of the Lane Gang, a group of young men who, much to my surprise, included both African Americans and Cape Verdeans. Their territory was the Kempton/Cedar Street area. There was the older Lane Gang and the younger Lane Gang. If I went to the store, I had to walk right by where they hung out. You had a certain stature when you hung with the Lane Gang. Their reputation and the sense of belonging I got when I was with them drew me like a magnet. I soon became part of the crew.

As part of the Lane Gang, I saw myself as an outlaw, an outcast. I wore it like a sweater. I knew that I was society's outcast when they put me in Room 214, from my perspective, the toughest seventh grade class in the school, with the toughest teachers. I didn't understand why they put me in there. Up to that point, I didn't see myself as being tough.

No one expected me to do well in school, except in one class—I excelled in science. The teacher, Mr. Ward, was the only school teacher who saw that I had the ability to succeed in an academic way. I don't know if he realized the impact he had on me wanting to learn, but to this day, my desire to learn has roots in his science class.

When I stayed back in the seventh grade, I walked around all cocky like it was no big thing—even though I was embarrassed. At that point, the spirit to achieve something, to have a purpose, had basically been stomped out. And when I looked around me at my closest friends, many of them were like that. There was no brightness or "I want to do something with my life." It was like, this is the way it is, this is the way it's supposed to be, this is our fate. I didn't feel I had anywhere to go but lateral, that there was no upward movement for me.

School began to mean less and less to me. Dressing nice, getting a girlfriend, getting respect from my peers—those are the things that were important to me. I wasn't getting it at home or in school, so I went out on the street and got it from my friends: "Oh, he's tough. Oh, he's slick. Oh, he don't care. Did you see when he hit that guy?" Be the leader; I always wanted people to follow me—that is where I found my self-respect.

Others were proud because they were good in football, they did well in school, or their family had money and power. We were labeled as troublemakers and people who couldn't achieve, and we wore it as a badge of honor, almost. We had to create something in ourselves that we felt proud about.

That same year we moved to the West End, my younger sister Adeline died. She had heart disease and Down syndrome. Her death stirred up in me all those feelings again of being a bad person, that I had been responsible for killing my baby brother.

Some of the guys I hung out with drank Roma Port wine. I began to drink with them when I was fourteen. That was the first time that I medicated myself; I say *medicated*, because I hated the taste of it. But the alcohol quelled my soul, all the unrest going on inside me, and the fear of the unknown, not knowing where I was going. It was as natural to me as a baby crying, the mother comes and feeds the baby with the bottle and rocks the baby, making the baby feel better. By the time I reached tenth grade, I was drinking on a regular basis. I used to bring alcohol to school in my gym bag and, during lunch period, I would be drinking.

As a Cape Verdean, I was making the transition in better understanding who I was. I was no longer in the state of limbo "Well, I'm not Black, but I'm not white." When James Brown was singing, "Say it loud! I'm Black and I'm proud," we were saying we're *poor* Black and we're proud: "I'm Black, and the reason I'm so poor is because I'm Black. And the reason that I'm a failure is because that's the way it's supposed to be, but I don't give a fuck, because it don't mean nothing." I gained something from knowing where I fit into the bigger picture. But at the same time, I didn't think there was any way out.

We—not just my generation, but the generations before us—had been put down so long if someone from the community did something special, there were two reactions: surprise or jealousy. "What? He made it?" or "He ain't going to make it long." Their success challenged who we were and at times made us feel less than, so we sometimes attacked.

I always questioned, "Why is it like this?" I questioned it when I was a kid walking up Hawthorn Street, when I stayed back in seventh grade, when I saw Martin Luther King challenging discrimination in the South—"I know this is happening way down there, but what does that mean here?" When I was delivering papers one day in sixth grade, three white kids beat me up and called me a nigger. But I can count the times on my hands that I heard the word *nigger* growing up. The racism that we experienced in New Bedford was less obvious, but no less destructive to the soul than the blatant bigotry down South.

During the riots in the wake of Martin Luther King's assassination, the young Blacks in New Bedford followed suit. Without any real understanding of the oppression we were experiencing, I wanted to have power over something. I was never a big guy—small, especially at that age. But I was one of the more reactionary young men. When everybody was downtown milling around and talking about whether to riot or not, I was the first to pick up a rock and break a window. If we were getting ready to fight, who threw the first punch? I did. Because that was my only way of being able to make sense out of things and not feel completely powerless. The only power I thought I had was the power of destruction.

At that point, I began to see whites as my enemies. They're the ones who made my life as bad as it was. What I could do is act out against those white people closest to me, the buildings owned by whites that were closest to me. I was brutal. Whether the kid was bigger than me or not, I was never content with smacking somebody. I would try to hurt them. In junior high, I used to start fights against the football team—older, privileged, primarily white kids. I would walk by somebody and nudge him and then he'd say, "Who you pushing?" Then I'd hit the kid and that would start the fight.

I couldn't comprehend that what I was feeling was rage at the system. I was reacting to things like I had no sight. Like walking in a dark room and just reaching out, and if I bumped something, I'd cry, "Ow!" and I'd back up. I didn't have any way of negotiating how I would get through.

Most who considered themselves to be leaders in the Black community worked basically for their own self-interest. They would start out being real radical, but ended up what we called *poverty pimps* with well-paying, government-funded jobs and would quiet down. And when they quieted down, they expected the young people to quiet down. That was just the way it was supposed to be, because—don't forget—we were taught to respect our elders. So we would follow suit most of the time. It was only later that I saw that those so-called leaders were getting in the way of progress.

We had to look far away for role models. We looked up to people like Muhammad Ali. He was an awesome boxer and boxing is one of my favorite sports, but I was also impressed by his confidence and his ability to stand for what he believed in. The stand he took against going into the service and the war in Vietnam helped me to understand racism as a global issue.

There weren't many Black professionals in my community. I sometimes wonder what difference positive role models would have had in my life—how that might have affected the course of my life and where I'm at in terms of my understanding of who I am. I think young people who have worked closely with me over the years benefit from my life experience: some of the painful lessons that I've learned, soul-searching that I have done, and the vision that I see in terms of where we as human beings are heading.

3

Alternative Sentencing

In 1969, there was a lot of social unrest going on across the country. I was seventeen and getting more into the street life, hanging out and talking about our blackness, drinking and identifying what we thought was injustice done to us, until there was no separation of the two.

We would hang in a field we called the People's Park. Uncle Dudley used to come out sometimes at night with his Conga drums, a big sack of corn, and some pots. We would start a little fire, cook the corn up, be playing our Congas, and the police would come and say it's time to go home and we would say, "No, it ain't time to close shop"—especially the younger punks like me. And that would be the beginning of trouble. One time the police lined up on one side of the field facing north and we lined up on the other side facing south—like the Civil War. Jet Stream Smith, Manny Costa, and a few other people were in the middle telling us to go home and telling the cops to cool off. I was one of the people in the front talking shit, "Fuck that, we ain't going nowhere." Then the police swept across and arrested people.

One evening I was standing on the corner drinking with a group of friends and saw three young women walking down Kempton Street. They looked like they were white folks to us, so we were going to fuck with them. I had a blank pistol that night. I stuck it in the women's faces and told them to hand over their money. When they said, "We ain't got no money," we said, "Okay, get the hell out of here." We laughed about it, not thinking it was a big deal.

Two days later when I was walking down the street, Detective Gibson pulled up alongside me, screeching his brakes, jumped out of the car, threw me against a wall, and told me I was under arrest for attempted armed robbery. He was a big Black officer who we saw as an Uncle Tom, as wanting to be part of the establishment.

Down at the police station, they roughed me up bad. I got bailed out and by the time the case went to court, it was almost midsummer. The court-appointed lawyer told me he had talked to the prosecuting attorney and could probably guarantee that he wouldn't prosecute me if I went into the service. The government was looking to communities of color for young men to send over to fight in Vietnam. It was the familiar story of old white men making decisions about young people of color.

One of my brothers was in the Marines and another was in the Army. When they came home, I used to look up to them; they had a certain stature with their uniforms on. When the court basically told me you can go to jail or you can go in the service, I enlisted in the Army in August 1969 for what was supposed to be three years. In my basic training at Fort Dix, New Jersey, I was struck that the drill instructors were mostly Black. I remember looking at them standing there so proud and strong. Even the specialists who did the training—they called them *Spec-4s* and most of them had been in Vietnam—were primarily Black too. I'd never seen somebody Black with that type of authority who I thought I could respect and look up to.

In the Army, I felt like I belonged to something. I was impressed with the apparent power, control, and status of the drill instructors and I aspired to get some of that. I never felt like I had any of that outside of being in the Lane Gang and being on the street. At seventeen years old, I was not only the youngest in my company, but the smallest in height and weight. The only Cape Verdean. But in my eagerness, I always outdid everyone. They made me squad leader. There's nothing I've ever done in my life that I wanted to half-step in anyway. Whatever I do I always jump right in and they must have seen that drive and commitment. My eagerness to get into things was what they were looking for. I thought they were valuing me as a person.

Seventeen years old, with only eight weeks of basic training, I didn't understand the Vietnam War and volunteered to go because I had a brother who had served there. After basic training, I was sent to advanced individual training. My first choice when I had joined was to work in security with dogs, because I always loved animals. I saw myself going on missions in Vietnam with a German shepherd. My second choice was to be in supply, because I heard there was a lot of money to be made if you were in supply over in Vietnam. You could get stuff and sell it—so there was that mentality going on too. I got my second choice—to be a clerk in supply.

On my way to advanced individual training at Fort Jackson in Columbia, South Carolina, the bus driver got lost in Virginia near the North Carolina border. It was raining hard, and we ended up off the main road, driving down a back road with nothing but fields on both sides and little shacks about the size of a one-car garage strung out along the road. On the steps were Black folk. Looking into their faces, I could feel a lifetime of pain, of hopelessness, of despair. I had never seen that level of poverty. I saw so many poor Black folks as we were riding down that road that it began to hurt, right in my chest.

That feeling that I used to have about inequality came back. I was so angry, but, at the same time, so, so sad that for the rest of the trip I was within myself, with a lump in my throat, thinking about all the feelings I had growing up, feeling like I wasn't worth much, that I had pushed underground with alcohol and hanging out: look what they do to Black people in this country.

When we got off the bus at Fort Jackson and took our bags to the barracks, the first thing I did was call home. I talked to my mother and my father and cried like a baby about what I had seen. I couldn't believe that people lived like that—like slaves and, in a big way, that's what they were. My mother heard my pain. My father stood away from it—he had been down South as a serviceman and had been called a nigger and what I was saying probably brought up those feelings he buried once he got back to New Bedford. Growing up in New Bedford, he saw himself as being Portuguese, he was Cape Verdean, he was different.

Caught up in the Cape Verdean culture, I also had bought into the idea that I was different. Even in basic training in New Jersey, I wanted to believe that a distinction was made between me and other people of color. Even though we were singing "I'm Black and I'm proud," I hadn't moved beyond that thought that I was a little bit better off than they were.

But down South, I clearly saw that I was a Black man. In Columbia, South Carolina, I could see how people looked at me, how they stared at me, how they talked to me, that they didn't make a distinction. That's when I knew there was no difference between Cape Verdeans and African Americans, that we were just people who had landed in this country different ways. The reality of our lives was no different. I saw the white race as being the oppressor, the enemy. I was on a level of pure hatred based on skin color. Going through advanced individual training, I went into town only once or twice. I felt safer on base.

But I still wanted to go to Vietnam to go fight. When the training was done, they said no, you're going to Germany. I was upset, thinking, "Man, they screwed me twice." First, I had wanted to go into dog training and security, because I was picturing down the road that I could do that for a living—they denied me that. Now I wanted to go to Vietnam and they denied me that. That sense of power that I thought I was gaining, I realized you don't really have any power. And even those people that you were looking up to, they don't have any control either.

In December of '69, I was sent to Germany and got swept up with the excitement of going to another country. When I landed in Germany, they were looking for volunteers to serve as unit police—it wasn't full military police. I thought it would give me a chance to do security. What sold me was that unit police were on duty twenty-four hours straight, then off for forty-eight.

In the unit police, I made friends with Dennis Young, we called him "Detroit," George Nobles from Chicago, Therman Keene from Philadelphia, and a guy from Puerto Rico. He was the first Hispanic that I knew as a friend. When he told me, "We're a part of the United States, but we can't vote," I said, "Wow! How could someone end up in the armed forces fighting for this country, but they can't decide on who's the President?" I saw how the United States had its thumb on them and made the connection between their situation and what we Blacks in America were going through.

They were all big city people and not used to being cramped in. I was the youngest and from a small city, so they took me under their wing. Working the same shift gave us two days to do what we wanted to after that one day of work. We were always on the move, going to different barracks and different towns.

I had been stirred awake by going down South and there I was in Germany feeling racism at a different level. I saw how German television programs portrayed American Blacks in the ghettos as inhuman. Just as there was a lot of racial strife going on back in the U.S., there were major problems between the Black and white servicemen, racial acting out by the white servicemen and Blacks, especially those who had been to Vietnam, trying to show some self-identity. In Vietnam, Blacks saw themselves as having some power, challenging the armed forces in terms of being able to wear an Afro and crosses that we used to make out of boot strings. They had grasped on some level what was going on in Vietnam in terms of people of color being asked to kill other people of color. I met people who identified as Panthers—who I later learned were considered renegades, because they were no longer under the leadership of the Panther Party—who furthered my understanding of oppression and the class war. I became radicalized in my opinions about the war, the role we played as Black servicemen, and how we were treated differently. I felt like a patsy and no longer wanted to be playing that part.

In July 1970, I was sitting in the barbershop getting a haircut, listening to the Stars and Stripes radio program and, over the airways, they talked about a riot in New Bedford, Massachusetts. My buddies said, "Hey, New Bedford, that's your town!" Everybody stopped and listened: the news report said four people had got shot and one was killed. They broadcast the names of the people who had been shot and one was Ribeiro. I said that was it, I don't belong here. There are people back home getting killed. Why was I here in Germany when back home was where the struggle was happening?

I went right over to my CO's office. He had been wounded in Vietnam and walked with a limp. I said to him, "I want to get out of the service. I don't want to be here no more." He laughed at me and said, "You can't quit." I went on about how I didn't want to be a puppet and wanted to be back in the United States because one of my family members had got shot and other people I knew. He said that he was going to make a man out of me, that I was not there to quit.

From that moment on, I was a thorn in their side. I let my hair grow. I didn't blouse my boots. I just dressed the way I wanted to. I got to the point where I wasn't even saluting officers. I would just walk right by them like they were nobody.

We could have Afros at that point, though it could be only a certain number of inches high and had to be so many inches away from the ear. An official who was studying the racial problem in the armed forces over there held a town meeting, so to speak, in my barracks. I stood up and asked did my hair fit under the new regulations. When he said yes, my CO jumped up from the other side of the room and threatened me in front of everyone: "Ribeiro, I'm sick of your stuff! I told you that I was going to make a man out of you and I'm not done with you yet!"

The Panthers had told me that if we wanted to leave Germany, all we had to do was get to Sweden, which took a neutral stand on the Vietnam War, and the Panthers would make arrangements to get us back from there to the United States. Talking someone we knew in Headquarters Company into giving us fake orders, Dennis, George, Therman, and I set out in our Volkswagen for Sweden. From Denmark, we took a ferry over to Sweden. Walking to where a big anti-war rally was being held, we saw people running toward us. When we stopped someone to ask what was going on, he said that the Swedish police were making a raid, checking the papers of any American, and anybody that was there illegally was going to get sent back under lock and key to Germany. We'd probably end up getting sent to Fort Leavenworth as deserters, since this was during wartime. Getting back to the car, we snuck back over to Denmark and back to Germany.

I got back to my company in late evening. Early the next morning my CO woke me with his .45 pointed at my head. He arrested me and they sent me to what was basically a prison. Ninety percent of the people there were Black, and I heard horror stories of people who had been there for months without a trial.

My buddies had a different relationship with their CO and simply got disciplined within their company. To see that I got some type of justice, they went around with a petition to all the different barracks and collected signatures saying that I was a political prisoner and someone needed to look into my case, because my CO had it out for me. They sent these letters back to the United States to my mother, who took them to her state representative.

I was in there for about a month when the same person who had been studying the racial unrest there was making a tour through the prison. I screamed his name out. He heard me, came up to the cell and I recalled the town meeting where my CO said he was going to get me. I said, "Well, he ended up getting me." He said, "Do you want to get out of here?" I said, "Yeah." He said, "Well, I'm going to help you do that."

The next day a warrant officer, who is like a lawyer, said, "You sign this paper, we can get you out under honorable conditions," which means you get all your benefits. I signed it and twenty-four hours later, I was getting off the plane in New York. I was back in New Bedford that same day and went right over to the Panther headquarters.

4

Liberated Territory

Responding to the racial unrest in the city, the Black Panther Party had set up shop under the name *National Committee to Combat Fascism* on the corner of Kempton and Cottage Streets, my old territory. My older brother Bruce had talked to them about me, what I was doing out in Germany, and how I wanted to get involved.

I got out of the service in October 1970. My brother-in-law Reggie and my father picked me up at the Boston airport. All the way coming back home, I said, "I can't wait to meet these people." Back in New Bedford, I brought my bags to my mother's house, kissed my mother, ate some *jag⁷*, stayed home for about an hour, and went right over to the Panther Party headquarters. When I walked into the NCCF building, I felt right away that was where I needed to be. The next day I started to attend their political education classes, where we read Mao Tse-tung's *Red Book* and the teachings of Malcolm X.

I would wake up, go to the headquarters, and spend the whole day there. Thinking they had taken control of my mind, my mother got in touch with Reverend Chavier, who took me out for lunch the fourth day I was back in the city. He was someone who I respected, for he had made me feel like I had some self-worth. So, out of respect for him, I met him for lunch. Throughout the conversation, he pictured the role I could play within the church—that I was a leader and I could be a minister or missionary. I kept bringing it back to what was going on right now in this community—how months ago Lester Lima, who was also a member of the church, got killed and the people responsible weren't even going to jail for it. Something needed to be done about that. That's where we clashed. By the time we got through talking, he told my mother, "At this point, there's nothing we can do for him." I was considered a lost cause, someone who was completely brainwashed.

A day or two after that I moved out of my house into the Panther Party headquarters. I got very involved in the political education classes and helped run the free breakfast program. Of the fifteen or so members of the Panther Party in the city, about half were from outside the area and half from New Bedford. But there was a broader community of people who supported what the Panther Party was doing and stood for. We had what we called Panther Party Kids who came to the free breakfast program every morning and we would sing songs with them about Black pride and unity.

Three or four of us would go to the businesses downtown and ask for donations for the free breakfast and free clothing programs. Because of my hard looks, the Panther leadership used to say, "You just stand there and give that stare." I used to just stand off in the corner and stare the gangster look. The head cadre told me I taught people more through what I did than what I said. Back then I saw value in that and was happy with that role I could play. During the year I was involved with the Panthers, my self-esteem grew.

That I had gone out of the country and seen things in a broader way gave me a different understanding than a lot of local folks who hadn't seen the things I had: going down South and experiencing the racism down there, being in the military where they try to chop you down and build you up, being in Germany and seeing racism at the international level. I was able to talk to the Lane Gang genre about my experiences because I was putting it out to them not as someone from another community or someone using fifty-cent words; I was able to say it in the way we talked.

The Panther Party experience helped me to see the bigger picture: what the Vietnamese people were fighting for was no different from what the people staging sit-ins down South were struggling for. The role that the police department played in communities across this country was no different from the role that the U.S. Army and Marines played overseas. The Panthers helped me to understand the struggle we were involved in wasn't just about race. I learned about the historical connections between the anti-slavery movement, the women's suffrage movement, the civil rights movement we were involved in, and elderly people's struggle for their rights. It boiled down to the issue of people being denied basic human rights based on the color of their skin, their class background, gender, their sexual identity, or age.

The Panthers helped me to understand that oppression breeds resistance, that we can organize and do something about it, and that doing something meant that you had to have discipline, you had to have a vision, and you had to get involved in the political process. They taught me any fundamental change had to happen from the bottom up. Whenever you have a revolution that doesn't begin with the people who are the most disenfranchised, if it doesn't include them in creating the vision of what that change should look like, if it doesn't include them in strat-egizing and bringing about the change, then you don't have a base for real change to happen. There are many lessons from history where so-called revolutions have happened, but nothing has changed in terms of what goes on in that country. You still have social stratification where you have poor people and rich people, people with power and people without power.

The Panthers stressed that individuals and communities should have the power of self-determination, to be able to decide what they wanted to be. The right of communities to decide their own futures struck a responsive chord in me. I thought my role could be to create some type of avenue to make that happen in New Bedford.

We were thinking that an armed struggle was close to happening and that the Panthers would be at the vanguard of that. Across the country, Panther Party officers were getting ambushed. Huey Newton had issued a directive "No pig is supposed to cross our threshold, no matter what."[8] We held liberated territory.

We expected at some point the police would come in and we would have a shootout. At our headquarters, the door was a foot thick with sand packed in the middle and the whole first floor was fortified with sandbags like a fort. One evening we got word that the police were going to raid us. Michael Early and I stayed in the building, while everyone else formed a perimeter around the build-ing. I was on the first floor with a single-barrel pump-action shotgun that could hold eight shells and an ammo box full of shotgun shells. Michael was up on the third floor with an AK47. We were there for about two or three hours that evening, and I stood there, very quiet, all the lights out in the house, protecting this one doorway on the Cottage Street side of the house, just waiting. In my mind, revolution was about to happen, and I was going to be a part of it, and I was prepared to die. The police never raided the place, though a number of times late at night people came by and shot into the building. We figured it was the police trying to scare us so as to chase the Panthers out of the city.

I started developing my own vision beyond what the Panthers were teaching and challenged them on the contradictions I saw. Concerning the issue of drugs, a lot of the Panthers were smoking reefer. It was part of our culture even though they were against drug dealing, especially the hard drugs like heroin and cocaine.

The Panthers had a special dislike of pimps and tolerated them less than drug dealers. Even though the Panthers talked a good talk about sexism and women being equal, I saw that men were in most positions of authority. I didn't feel comfortable with the unspoken rule that men could have sex with as many of the women as they wanted to. Although this worked both ways at times, it seemed that men used their positions of power to get women to have sex with them. The Panthers preached equality, but the Party seemed to become more stratified.

In 1971, divisions within the Panther Party led to a lot of chapters closing down or breaking off. The New Bedford chapter shut down in early May 1972. Everybody was supposed to go work in the Boston chapter. I decided to stay and put what I had learned into action. I had a vision of developing a political and economic base in the West End of the city. Another reason for staying was Susan, a Panther Party supporter who became my wife and the mother of my first two children.

Susan's stepfather, John Cruz, also a supporter of the Panther Party, helped found the United Front in New Bedford in early May 1968. Continuing on into the 1970s, the United Front called for better housing, health care, and other services for the West End community.[9] Martin Luther King's success in negotiating was in part because the white establishment realized they had to negotiate with him or reckon with the more radical groups like the Panthers. That also happened on the local level. In New Bedford, the less radical groups like the United Front and the NAACP were able to win some gains partly because of the Panthers' presence in the city.

5

The End Doesn't Justify the Means

In 1971, Susan gave birth to our first child, a boy. I wanted to be with them so much that, although I didn't believe in the legal institution of marriage, we decided to marry. The Panther Party stressed the importance of children and I bought into the concept of being a father. I had visions of him and me being involved with the movement together when he grew older.

I named him after George Jackson's younger brother, Jonathan Jackson, who tried to free three Black prisoners on trial in San Rafael, California for assaulting a guard. Just seventeen years old, Jonathan made a one-man raid on the court-house, armed the prisoners, and took five hostages, including the assistant district attorney and the judge. They made it all the way down to a van being used for the getaway when the police shot the van up and Jonathan Jackson, two prisoners, and the judge were killed.

Seeing Jonathan Jackson as a hero, I named my son Jonathan Ulysses Ribeiro. The name *Ulysses* was after a man named Ulysses I read about in the Panther Party newspaper who was in jail for twenty-something years, with over half that time in solitary confinement. The brother had a strong spirit and never lost touch with reality. The Panther Party newspaper ran articles about him and printed messages he sent out to the people.

I read George Jackson's book *Blood in My Eye*, where he talked about going to school and learning things in the way that the oppressor did, because the only way you could deal with them was to understand how they thought. He talked about the need to train engineers, doctors, lawyers, law enforcement people, all of those professions needed to build a better society.

As a veteran, I could get money to go to school. A cousin who was a registered nurse sold me on the idea of enrolling in the nursing program at the local univer-sity. Although I went with good intentions, I didn't have my GED and wasn't prepared. My cousin tried to help me, but I didn't have the fundamentals or the study skills to get through even the easiest classes.

I wasn't emotionally prepared either. I had the same feelings I had just before I left high school. I was searching for something, but didn't know what it was. I knew I wanted to do something in life, I wanted to succeed in something, but didn't have a clear plan of what that was. I ended up spending most of my time shooting pool and dropped out the next semester.

Reading *Blood in My Eye*, I thought about starting a business and through this business creating some economic strength in the Black community. Starting the business for me was tied into the whole social change concept, even though I understood that capitalism as an economic system was destined to eat itself up. While I knew that capitalism was going to collapse, you needed to promote something to replace it. I envisioned that what I was starting in New Bedford would be part of that something to replace the current system.

I decided to set up a record shop that carried Black music. I was living on the first floor of the house owned by my brother-in-law Reggie, who was dealing drugs. Knowing he had money, I started talking to him and to a friend who had been involved with the Panthers about going into business with me. I related my vision of getting this record shop up and running, starting to make some money, and then one of us could run for City Council. They bought the idea; we got a building on Kempton Street and opened West End Records. My older brother Richie, who was also a drug dealer, came in with some money and became the fourth member of the corporation. We used to go up to Skippy White's in Boston, bring records back, and sell them. While it had a niche as the only Black-owned record store in the city, the business struggled.

During the late sixties, early seventies, drugs flooded into the community, like other poor communities of color across the country, and became a major part of the culture. I saw the drug trade flourishing all around me. Doing the record business with people who were involved with the drug economy, I saw the amount of money that Richie and Reggie were making.

It was much easier for anybody in our community who had even a little bit of entrepreneurship to get involved with the drug trade than to open a legal business. I had no clear path, no role models before me who had opened up businesses. To deal drugs, all you had to do was have the want to do it and it was available to you.

As much as I knew it was against my Panther Party training, I began weighing the idea of getting involved with drug dealing for maybe six months to make money at a faster rate in order to do some of the progressive things that I wanted to do. I didn't respect the law. I saw it as a tool that was used against people of color. During that period, we were breaking into houses where we knew there were guns and building up a cache of guns and ammo, because we believed there was going to be a war. We saw ourselves as the underground liberation army in the area.

So to do something that was illegal was not at all a stretch for me. Being a person of color and poor, I believed that we had to survive *by any means necessary* [Malcolm X], though I knew that selling drugs in my community was wrong.

Susan and I agonized about it for weeks. One Saturday afternoon we were standing in front of the record store closing up, we looked at each other, and I said, "Let's do it, because there's all kinds of money in it. All they're doing is pumping the money back into the drugs, but we can do something positive with it." Sometimes you take two steps back in order to take three steps forward—being young and inexperienced, we thought that the end would justify the means, that we could get involved with the drug trade for a short period of time, raise some quick money, and justify it because it was going to help with this process of change.

My brother Richie was my role model as a drug dealer in terms of how he carried himself, how he dressed, how he talked to people very gentlemanlike, and how he always had girlfriends. To start off, Richie would give me some cocaine and say, "When my customers come by, if I'm not around, you just take care of them." About a month into doing this, he called me up, "Hey, I've got something in my house that I've had stashed for a long time and I'm not doing nothing with it. Why don't you take it." I went over to the house and he gave me a pound of reefer.

I started selling reefer and hooked up with a couple of good friends—one who was my best friend who had just got back from Vietnam. Because I was business- and organization-minded, our reefer business quickly became the biggest in the West End and expanded to the South End. We used to sell the reefer with a pack of papers taped to it, so customers knew who they got it from. We eventually got big enough that we would buy like five, six pounds at a time, make bags out of it, and have other people sell it. Eventually we got into selling pounds.

Living that life on the street, you always have to worry about sooner or later getting caught. What I had that Reggie and the others involved in the drug dealing part of the business lacked was security consciousness. The Panthers had taught me security. I brought that to the business of selling drugs. They would call me Mr. Paranoia. One of the rules I had was don't carry drugs. Don't keep drugs at your house. We started getting apartments all through the city where we would stash our drugs.

Some of those survival traits are still engrained in me. I still always make sure my doors are locked. I'm the one that puts the shades up and down in my house. Even though I'm not doing anything wrong, it's a habit from being in the streets all those years that you always want to protect what you're doing.

Eventually instead of being just a bit partner in the drug operation, I became a major player. We brought in two more partners—a guy from Chicago and another from Detroit; they had been in the service with my brother-in-law. We became well known in both the addict community and the law enforcement community as being the main drug dealers in the West End and pretty well established throughout the city. Although Reggie and his friends were much more visible, there was no doubt that I was connected with it. I just conducted myself in a different way. They all had big, flashy cars. Reggie had a black, fancy Cadillac that was maybe one of a hundred made and definitely stuck out in the city. I didn't have a fancy car until '76, when I bought a Cadillac Brougham.

In the first two years of the legal business, we branched out into a luncheonette I bought on Hillman Street. It was named West End Luncheonette, but nicknamed Harry O's by the clientele. We would keep it open till three in the morning for the late night crowd. We sold all kinds of food, *jag* and all that, and it became the place to go to when the nightclubs closed. We eventually turned half the record shop into a variety store. Then we opened up a nightclub in the North End called The Devil's Den and brought in live entertainment from Boston, New York, and other places.

My partners and I became so big that we affected the cost of drugs in southeastern Massachusetts. If people sold drugs lower than us, Reggie used to make a trip to go find them and convince them to conform to our wishes. I had said to Susan, "We'll do it for a little while, and then we'll get out." Then I got bit by the Superfly Syndrome.

6

Legend

Violence was part of being a successful drug dealer. One night in early summer of 1972 we were told that some guys from Providence had just kidnapped Ron and my brother Bruce and were holding them for ransom because they wanted to get money off my partners and me. They thought Ron and Bruce were part of the crew, though they just hung out and got high with us.

Will Smith and I jumped in a car to go find them. He had three cars at the time but the car he took was the fast one, the racing car. We each had a gun. We rode through the West End looking different places and as we were going by a parking lot, we noticed a car way in the back. When Will started to turn into the lot, they tore out of there. Will got in behind them, going right through stop signs. When they made a turn, Ron came flying out. He must have jumped out. We didn't stop to pick him up and kept chasing the car. Though we didn't know it, they had let Bruce go before they even took off with the intent of him going to get the money from the crew.

The car went up the street, down the street, and we were flying after them shooting. I can't believe to this day there were no cops around. My gun ran out of bullets and Will gave me his pistol and I kept firing at them. We chased them through the West End like Wild, Wild West up onto the highway for a couple of miles and finally their engine blew. They were ahead of us by about half of a football field. All of a sudden a billow of thick black smoke came flying back and engulfed our car and we had to slow down. By the time the smoke dissipated enough for us to see, they had pulled over in the breakdown lane and all we saw were sneakers running in the nighttime woods. The next day their car was at the State Police barracks on Route 6, all bullet holes in the back.

That was the first link in the chain of events that took hold of Ron and Legend. A couple of months later, I was having a party at my house when Ron came in and said, "Them guys that grabbed me and Bruce came into town and are down at the West End Social Club!" So we all ran back there. When I got to the

Social Club, they were coming out. I hit one, *boom, boom*, a couple of times. Ron hit him once or twice, but it wasn't a real fight because he wasn't fighting back. We were saying, "What the hell you coming into New Bedford? Stay out of town!"

It was a near riot feeling that summer night. Ron had a pistol in his hand and was talking with it. As he was talking and waving the gun, it went off by accident. *Bang!* Everything completely stopped for a couple of seconds, but what seemed like a lifetime. Everything got quiet. I was three feet away from the guy who got shot. He didn't fall, just backed up against the wall, and held his chest. He was fully conscious; we didn't see any wound. Once everybody saw that, somebody kicked the other guy and told him, "Get the hell out of here and don't come back no more!" He started to run for his car. The guy who got shot took one or two steps toward the street, groaned, and fell down.

The women started screaming and everybody ran. We went to the house of a girl that we hung out with, there must have been about ten of us. We were all scared because it was the first time we had seen somebody get shot. We were there for about an hour when a friend came in and said, "Hey, that guy died." There was a lot of emotion running through us, the biggest being fear.

That night the police began to round up people. They did a house-to-house search in the area. For two or three days, they just grabbed people off the street and arrested them. They arrested this guy called Jughead, who used to do odd jobs for us. He was stocky with short hair and they said he was the guy that hit and kicked the guy. They were trying to make it look like this had happened after he got shot and charged Jughead with murder. I didn't come out on the street for a week. I didn't even stay home. I was scared shitless, because every day I'm reading the newspaper and seeing pictures of people I knew on the front page.

They got Ron that night. They also arrested his brother Legend that night in front of his house. They ended up charging four people, two were acquitted during the trial, and it came down to just Ron and Legend.

Because they had arrested Legend saying he had done the shooting when we knew he didn't, the lawyers felt like it's not a good time to come up and say anything yet, let's let them go with this. The thought was that they could beat it, because the police had the wrong man. Legend wasn't even there that night. In the trial, the lawyer never used me as a witness, and before you know it, they had found Legend guilty of first-degree murder and sentenced him to life in prison without parole. Ron was also given a life term, but with the chance of parole.

I met Legend when I was a kid. He was one of the tough guys who inspired both respect and fear in the West End community. Like a lot of other Black men, he ended up a grunt in Vietnam, and like a lot of others, he was probably suffering from PTSD [post traumatic stress disorder].

I got to know Legend at a much more intimate level when I came back from the service and joined the Panther Party. He was one of the "New Bedford Twenty"—people who were arrested in the July 1970 raid as the instigators of the 1969 riots.[10] He worried both the white and Black establishment. Legend definitely saw himself as being in a war; a lot of us did. Our mentality was that the revolution had come. It was just a matter of time that it was going to be at the level where people would be dying on both sides as opposed to just Black folks getting killed.

Legend had a charisma about him, a gift to lead people. His leadership was based on his ability to, as they would say on the street, *get over* on the system by not getting arrested at times. People followed him based on his strength in terms of his ability to throw down, but also his quick thinking that won arguments. I felt a sense of power when I was with him because he acted so powerful. I was in situations with Legend where we were the only two African Americans in a Spanish bar or a poor white Fall River neighborhood, and Legend would do some shit that would probably get any other two guys beat to death. He would stare people down and his fearlessness oozed out of him that people would like, "Wait a minute, should I mess with this guy or just let him alone?"

Legend was all of five feet, seven inches and weighed maybe a hundred forty pounds. A nice looking Black man, Cape Verdean, he had these big fists—hands that seemed twice the normal size you would picture on somebody his height and weight. He looked like a warrior; he had big knuckles and his hands were always scarred up, rugged looking. And he was tough—you talk about Timex take a licking and keep on ticking? That was Legend. I was with Legend when there were seven or eight policemen with him handcuffed and they would have a hard time maintaining him. There were times the police would take him down to the cell and be beating him and you'd be saying, "What the hell is going on? How can that guy still be talking shit to them?"

Legend spent twelve years in prison for a murder that he didn't commit. It would be one thing if he was on the scene so he had something to do with it, but he wasn't even in that part of the city. I know that, because I was there. And the police and the lawyers knew he wasn't there because they heard it from enough people. Everybody knew it. It was so well known that the only conclusion you could come to about him getting convicted and being locked down that many years was that they wanted him off the street. Based on his color and his politics, he was seen as a threat. Based on his courage and his forcefulness, he was seen as a threat. So the criminal justice system did what they do to people that the status quo fears. When they can't get rid of them in any other way, they lock them up. When they ended up letting him out after all those years in prison, there were no big headlines, "Legend Found Innocent of Murder Charges." No, it was done with little fanfare.

There was a whole movement to free Legend. He went for retrial a couple of times and was defeated. In the appeal process, I testified for Legend up in Boston relating to him not being there. The defense lawyer came up to me after and said, "You did a great job. You were so believable." The defense team was sure that Legend was going to get off that time. But it was another two or three years before he was released, with the thought that they were going to retry him. They just never took steps to either clear him or retry him.

Imagine what it was like for him, for anybody to be locked up that many years and be innocent, and have the awareness to know the real reason why they're in there. It solidified in his mind everything that he thought about the system, about the war in Vietnam, about the riots. It did for me. I could never trust the criminal justice system. If we had a death penalty in this state, Legend could have been executed. They could have put an innocent man to death when we all knew without a doubt that he was innocent. How many cases are there like that right now? What must that do to a community in terms of taking away their heart, their ability to even think they could struggle against something?

The struggles that Legend later got involved in were his battle against that system that basically crushed him. He fought all these little battles, and he fought them in a way where it was like guerrilla warfare, in a sense that he didn't get involved in any extended battle in terms of creating an organization that's got a long-term plan. Like when we had a couple of killings in the West End, the issue itself and Legend being who he was, he could have started a campaign that would have helped solidify some of the movement work in the community. He would come down, speak at a rally, come across fiery, outspoken, get people fired up, and then he'd be off and you didn't know where Legend was, but he was probably off fighting another little struggle in another setting in another community. Maybe he did that because it made him feel better, made him feel like he was doing something, that he was fighting the struggle, that he was not a victim. And in between those times, he was self-medicating, because of his inability to cope with all the things that happened to him. Between growing up in the way that he did in the time that he did, going to Vietnam, being involved with the Panthers, and then going to jail for twelve years for a crime that he didn't commit, I think it taxed his coping mechanism. In my estimation, Legend was dealing with PTSD from not just the Vietnam War, but the war that we face on a daily basis in this country for human rights, in dealing with the oppression by those people who seek to keep the status quo. For one person to have taken as much as he did, the effect of that is what we saw—someone who had much experience, who still had the ability to lead, but was reactive in terms of how he dealt with things in his own life and when he got involved with issues. But no matter what he did or didn't do, I still respect the warrior in him. I still admire his strength and his ability to endure all that he did and not be silenced.

7

Superfly Syndrome

When I made that transition from being someone who had a vision of social change and then getting involved with drugs through naïve thinking, I fell into what I call the *Superfly Syndrome. Superfly,* one of the Black exploitation films of that time, promoted the character Superfly as a kind of Robin Hood because he helped people even though he was involved in drug use, dealing, and pimping. Like many other young people of color my age at that time, I bought the concept and ran with it. I modeled that person who, even though I'm selling drugs, I'm helping the community like sometimes helping people put food on the table.

I went from this person who was a child who was going to be a preacher, a missionary, who cried when Martin Luther King got killed, who was in the streets throwing rocks when Malcolm X got killed, who got involved in the Panther Party movement. When the Panther Party talked about the negatives in the Black community, besides the white businessman and the police, there were two groups of people that they felt strongly against: drug dealers and pimps. But I never once questioned that what I was doing was wrong.

People don't understand the power of drugs and the culture of drugs—what it does to a person's mental state, their ego, their soul. Take that action of selling drugs and having what you perceive as power, and then you add drug use that distorts your perception of things, unnatural things became natural for me to do.

As a drug dealer at twenty-two, twenty-three years old, I thought it was natural for me to be violent to somebody to get the money they owed me. I thought it was natural for me to be a drug dealer who had all these women at his beck and call. The culture, the media, and being in the service taught me to think that it was natural for me to try to get power over others as opposed to sharing power with. Once you buy into that lifestyle, it becomes a drug in and of itself. I got caught up into the drug of moneymaking, status, power, the competitiveness, being competitive with other people in the community who are dealing and dealing better than them.

As someone who always tried to be the best he could, I was good at selling drugs. I was good at creating an organization that dealt drugs. One of the reasons why I had begun to deal drugs in the first place was that the record shop wasn't sustaining itself. So now I was able to pump money into the business. Within a year, I as a twenty-three-year-old Black man owned businesses, had a nice big car, had apartments all over the city, had many girlfriends—everything that the media, that this consumption culture teaches you to want, I had. With drug money, I was able to be everything that society tells you that you want to be: have money, have power, have control, have people look up to you. And still that part of me says I could help people. So all those needs in me were, in a perverse way, being met through dealing drugs.

I bought into a very Western civilization-type thinking—the drive for immediate gratification. I could come and go as I pleased, I had no boss, I was good at what I did, so the police used to chase me and never catch me. I thought I had it together. What I saw? *Superfly* on the screen. I saw Superfly who did whatever he did and then in the end he walked away into the sunset and was free. That *was* me, that's what I thought I lived.

I put out this positive image. I dealt with people in a way that I thought was fair, upfront. People knew what I did. It was a business, like the liquor store down the street. It was so much of the culture of the community that many people accepted it. They saw me as the owner of the West End Variety Store, where they'd come and get credit. Many times the reason why I didn't get arrested was because some neighbor would call me.

My mother stayed in touch throughout that period when I was a dealer. She would try to get me to go to church and was hopeful that I would change my life around. "What you're doing, it's not right," she would say. "It's not helping people," and "You should find a job doing something else." I would tell her straight out, "This is what I do." Sometimes I wouldn't say anything, would just listen, because I knew what she was saying was right.

I bought a trained attack dog, a big German shepherd, that saved me from getting arrested a couple of times. I used Ajax more for the fear factor of having him. There were times I used to send him after people, but I always stopped him before he bit anybody.

I lived on the first floor; my sister and my brother-in-law Reggie, my main partner, lived on the second. One day when my sister was on her way out the door, the police were right there and burst in to raid the house. Ajax was standing in the first room, where there was a pool table. When the police saw Ajax, they backed up, giving me a couple of seconds to run back to the middle room. We were selling drugs out of the house that day and on the bar, we had all the drugs on a big plate, with a pile of heroin on one side and a pile of cocaine on the other and people would come in and if they wanted fifty dollars worth, you just made the bag up. It was easier to get rid of that way. I grabbed the plate and ran to the bathroom and put the water on to wash it off.

Just when I had finished and was coming out of the bathroom, Turcotte, who was head of the narcs at the time, came in through the back door. Trained as a personal protection dog, Ajax came back to me and saw Turcotte. When Turcotte went to grab me, Ajax lunged toward him. Out of the corner of my eye I saw him going and I reached to grab him, my hand hooked on the collar and I was able to stop him. Turcotte was backing up and reaching for his gun. Ajax was trying to grab him, but I was holding him, finally put him down, and told him to sit. Turcotte wanted to shoot him, but I said, "You ain't going to shoot him" and took him outside so he wouldn't shoot him.

Two weeks later the DEA [Drug Enforcement Agency] made a major raid in the city. They had warrants throughout the city. They were making a big deal about it, capturing the whole thing on television, the cops getting ready at the police station, getting into their cars, then all of a sudden, the TV camera showed that they were at my house, 65 Spruce Street, showed them hiding behind the high bushes in front of the house. Then it showed about ten of them in a big line running up the stairs with a battering ram and they went *wham*, then the tape goes off. My outside front door had this big window, almost half the door, then the rest of it was wood. They went for the glass, not knowing it was Plexiglas and the battering ram bounced off it. The next thing you see on tape, they're in the door, because they went down to the wood when they realized the window was Plexiglas. It was funny watching them on the news that night coming to the house, and *wham*, here goes the battering ram. It looked like the Keystone Cops.

The first thing the DEA agent said to me was "Where's that fuckin' dog? We heard about him and we're going to shoot him." I said, "Well, you can't shoot him, 'cause he's outside in his kennel in the yard." They didn't find anything, because we had got word they were coming.

We all had nice cars and were living what we thought was the life. A year or two into dealing I started to snort coke every now and then. I was using marijuana, snorting coke recreationally, and drinking alcohol.

In February 1974, Richie got killed. He was called over to a house to make a drug deal and, when he walked in with the guy, another guy came up behind him. My brother wasn't the type that if you put a gun to his face would say, "Okay, you got me." Apparently he made a motion to knock the gun out of the guy's hand and the guy shot him in the head. He died in the hospital within an hour.

I felt responsible for my brother's death, because I had gotten a phone call from somebody on the street that someone was going to rob him that day. Because I didn't give much creditability to the person who gave me the information, I didn't call my brother. To this day, I wonder if I had called him and told him, would he have done something different that day? Would he still be alive?

We never found out who killed him. But the police knew that I was looking for the other guy involved with my brother's murder. One day they chased me through the city streets trying to arrest me. A friend and I were in the car. I had a Buick Wildcat at the time. The chase lasted about ten minutes. I had a gun and drugs on me, made the corner, and threw the gun out and thought I threw the drugs out. They finally stopped us with a roadblock and searched the car. I got bailed out that night. The drugs were right on the car seat in a velvet bag, but because the car was black, they didn't find them.

As I look back on that period now, I believe that on some level it was supposed to happen that way, because no one can be that lucky. There were times when the cops would be right down the street, but someone just happened to see them. One time they caught me on the street and brought me to one of my apartments and searched it. The drugs were right there, but they didn't find them.

By 1976, none of my partners were on the street. My brother Richie was dead and Reggie, who was the godfather of our crew, and the others were all in jail. They got big time—seven years, ten years. I was the only one left.

Up to '76, I had gone out and bought the drugs only a few times. Reggie had the connections. Tom and Larry were the ones who did the copping. My head was more into security. With my partners in jail, I had to start making the runs to New York and other places to get the drugs. Taking the drive from New Bedford to New York to cop, people who have made this trip know that the toughest part of it was going through Connecticut. The Connecticut state police saw Route 95 as being the pipeline for drug couriers between New York and Connecticut, Rhode Island, and Massachusetts. And if they saw two or three Black men in a car, you can bet they were going to get stopped and searched.

Most of the time when I was on the highway during that period, I had drugs on me, I was copping, or I had money and was getting ready to cop, or I had my own personal use on me. But I've also been arrested for something when the police stopped me based on my color more than anything else. We people of color, especially men, are seen as suspects. I'm a suspect. I have a suspect look. Either he did something or he's getting ready to do something.

I still have that same fear that when they see me, that's what they see. So even now if I'm riding down the highway and I see the state police, my first reaction is an anxiety rush. If we go by them, I find myself looking in the rearview mirror to see if they're looking at me. I could be on my way to do a presentation at a school and the most dangerous thing I have on me is a pen and paper.

When I copped, I usually brought a heroin addict to try the drugs out. One day I made the run with somebody who wasn't a heroin addict and so I had to try it to make sure it was real dope. *Try it*, meaning I tasted it. I did that and then I took a snort in one nostril and then the other nostril, and I felt *damn!* Coming back from New York, I wasn't as nervous going through Connecticut. The next time I went up I did another couple of sniffs. Whenever I went to New York to go cop, I would take a couple of sniffs when I got there because I wouldn't be so high-strung coming back. I rationalized: you get high-strung you might not drive as straight, especially if the *staties* are out there. What was happening was my addiction was saying *feed me*.

After a while when we'd bring the drugs back, I would not only sniff out in New York, I started sniffing when we started to package the dope. When you get heroin, it's a certain percentage pure. The closer you are to the top of the food chain, the more pure the drugs are. Using milk sugar and quinine to cut my dope, I would make one ounce into four ounces—that's how you made your money on it. As we were cutting it, I would snort. Then I started snorting it before I went to New York.

Before I knew it, I was snorting heroin all the time. Wherever I went, I always had heroin in a little glass vial with me. Even in fancy restaurants, sitting there eating with people around, I would take out the vial with a little straw, cup it in my hand, and take a couple of sniffs. Go to the men's room if I had to. I always sat with my back to a wall, away from the center of things, so I could see what was coming at me all the time. I still have that habit when I go to a restaurant or a club.

I always thought that no matter what situation I was in, I could get myself out. Being medicated with the heroin, I had an ease that's not natural. Sometimes I carried a gun. But there were times I worried, especially where I had to go through a lot of addicts. They were robbing people just like I did later on when I was at my worst.

One place in New York where I copped was under a series of abandoned row houses. The people running the drug operation had knocked through all the cellar walls, so you would go underground five or six buildings over, maybe half a block, with no lights, through all kinds of bodyguards to where they were selling the drugs. Going in there with thousands of dollars, copping, and then having to walk back out—there was no guarantee that you would come out of there. One guy I knew went up there to cop and we never saw him again.

By 1976, not only had all my partners gone to jail and my brother got killed, but all the businesses closed down one after another, because now I was more into the street and getting high. The club was the first thing to go. Because Reggie was down as the President of the corporation, the liquor board took our license away. The luncheonette and variety store eventually closed and I got totally into dealing cocaine, heroin, and reefer.

8

Behind the Walls: Prince of the City

Because I was alert to what the cops were doing, I didn't get arrested until after four or five years of dealing. I was first arrested in 1976 when the police raided my home, where I lived with Susan and my two oldest kids. In the wee hours of the morning, the police used a battering ram to break my door down. We were sound asleep and all of a sudden, *balaaam!* I woke up scared stiff, not knowing who it was and what they were going to do to me and my family. I never even made it out of bed, that's how quick they got inside the house. They searched for a couple of hours, didn't find anything, then one cop found a little bit of cocaine I had given to my wife one time—it was like champagne back then—and she had put it in a jewelry box; it probably had been there months, just sitting there. Just a little bit in foil, not worth ten dollars, but they charged me with it.

I took my second arrest in '79 with one of my running partners. He used to deal the bags for me sometimes, but he was not a partner with the business. He was a good friend from my teenage years, my main hanging out buddy. He had some drugs on him and they put the drugs on me.

It was one of those times when I knew the police were on us. When I picked him up, I said, "Don't carry no drugs with you today, because I can feel it, I know we're going to get stopped." But he had it with him and said, "I just want to make one stop down the South End and drop it off." On the way down, the police pulled us over. He had it inside of a manila envelope. When we heard the siren and before they pulled us over, he threw it out of the car. They stopped us, searched us, didn't find anything. They were getting ready to leave when Turcotte, an older narc who had also chased my brother Richie for years, spotted it across on the sidewalk, walked over and picked it up. There were seven bags of heroin in it, and he said, "Got you, Ribeiro." I asked, "How you going to charge me with that?" He said, "Because I seen you throw it."

I was charged with possession with intent to distribute. Because it was my second drug charge, I was supposed to automatically get state time. I always saw the police as being the oppressor, that the court system was there to bury people—that their jobs were to keep the status quo. I always said I would never voluntarily give myself up. That day I went to court, my lawyer came back and told me, "They want to give you time. They're going to give you three to five." I was like, "They ain't giving me no time 'cause I'm out of here." That's why I never bought property. I had money and could have bought houses. All my partners bought houses. I didn't buy a house, because I always said in my mind, whenever it gets to that point where they're going to give me time, I'm gone. This country's too big; the only way I'll go to jail is if they physically grab me and put me in there. I will never walk in.

Standing on the Superior Court steps during lunch break, I was ready to go. Susan said, "Gerald, if you run, how are we going to do this? You're not going to be able to see the kids." I said, "You go with me," but she convinced me to go and do the time. I had a good lawyer who was able to get me a deal where I pleaded guilty and got instead two years at the county House of Correction, which meant with good behavior, I would be out in a year.

I went in March '79. My first night there I realized I was a full-fledged addict. I had been snorting $300-400 worth of heroin and cocaine a day. The medical officer gave me something the first night to get through it. I wasn't supposed to get it, but I knew him because he used to buy drugs off me on the street. The next day he brought in some methadone tablets—they were called *biscuits*—that people who worked for me gave to him for me. I hid them in my cell and weaned myself off the drugs. I went through two weeks of hell.

That first night in jail I had a claustrophobic attack. A lot of people go through that, especially your first time in there. In that cell late at night, twelve, one at night, the reality hit me, looking around me, little, little small-ass cell, I said, "Oh, my God, talk about being helpless. If there's a fire in here, who's to say they're going to let us out?"

But I knew a lot of the Black guards—people who bought drugs off me either for their own use or to sell on the street, knew their family. They took care of me, from bringing drugs in to bringing food—fried chicken, *jag*—off the street. Guards I knew from the street would sometimes stop by my cell if I was smoking a joint and take a toke or two.

In the House of Correction, you got out of your cell for breakfast and mid-morning for recreation, you were locked up until lunch, then you got out to eat lunch and got locked back up, you'd get out in the afternoon for a little while, then you ate supper, and then you were locked up for the rest of the night unless you had a color. A *color* meant you had a job. Depending on what job you had, you went out every other night—*go out* meaning to the recreation hall or to the place where they play cards and pool or to the gym. My first day I got a job: I was kitchen man, which gave me two colors and got me out every evening. Then I became the gym man. The gym man got out all the time.

Most every day I was in there, I got high. Because I didn't want to get hooked into it where I couldn't get anymore, I stood away from heroin. I did reefer, cocaine, and alcohol. Alcohol that was made in there, but mostly alcohol from the street—always 150 proof rum, because it was the most powerful.

Because the House of Correction was right in the middle of the West End, sometimes people would throw drugs in a ball over the wall. That wasn't that successful, because the guards would check around the perimeter of the jail before they let people out of their cells. Other ways were through visits; we used to cut holes in the screen between you and your visitor so visitors could stick the reefer joints through—sometimes cocaine or heroin, roll it up in paper small enough to slip it through. The prison officials would insert screws in the holes, but we would use screwdrivers to take the screws out, pass the drugs through, and put the screws back in.

I ran the gambling that went on in there and sold the reefer in there with a couple of my buddies. It was clear that the guards were the ones who ran the prison, but it wasn't so clear to the inmates who controlled the prison. Billy Souza, an officer or what we called a *white shirt*, hated me with a passion, because he knew the influence that I had over inmates and some guards, including guards who were in key positions. He would come to my cell sometimes and talk shit; I would talk shit back to him; he would yell and I'd yell through the bars. I would take it just to a point before he would say, "Open up this freakin' cell" and get his boys to come in there and kick my ass. I knew just how far to take it. Came close a couple of times, but was never put in isolation, never made that trip upstairs to the hole.

I was put in lockdown a couple of times, meaning you'd stay in your cell all day. It was not a big deal for me because I would stay high, watch TV all day, people would come by and drop me food.

Every now and then they'd do a shakedown—meaning they would do a raid on a particular cell, cell block, the whole prison—just to show that they had the power. You'd try to make your cell as comfortable as possible, because there was only a cot, a sink, and a little shelf to put your toiletry articles on. We used to hang pictures on the wall and get boxes, fancy them up, and make them like a little bureau. They would come through every two or three months and take all that away—they called that *contraband*. That would give them a reason to look for stuff or to lock somebody up.

You could have a TV, a radio, a tape deck as long as it couldn't record. Your TV was supposed to work by battery. But you always had someone who knew how to hook up into the electrical system. So I would take that down when they were going to do a shakedown.

I always knew ahead of time either from an inmate who found out from his contact or directly from one of the guards I knew. He would tell me, "Shakedown tomorrow afternoon. You got anything, give it to me, I'll bring it back to you." I made sure I never had anything in my cell when they came through.

When one of my friends would tell me, "Hey, man, come on. I got this young kid up here, he'll give you a blow job," I would get upset because I saw that as being a bully. Sometimes I tried to talk him out of it, "Man, come on, come on, don't do that, man, I mean we're only in here for a year." I couldn't condone that kind of oppression even back then. But it went on, and more than often I would just turn my back on it.

When you're in there, you need to have a crew. Even in a county prison doing short time, you don't want to be an individual, because people see that as a weakness and you can get jammed up. So I had my own crew, but with that I also had the respect of the larger population of people of color and a lot of the toughest white dudes from the Fall River area—people who used to come to New Bedford to buy drugs off of me—who were able to say to other Fall River guys that didn't know me, "You leave that man alone. You back off of him."

There was racial division going on in there big-time, especially with the white people from the Fall River area, who, with the poverty, had the street toughness of any one of us people of color, they could throw down with the best, had the same street attitude, the same cockiness, raw edge to their attitude. When there was some issue between a Black inmate and a white inmate, or sometimes bigger issues where a group of Blacks and a group of whites would be planning to have a big throwdown maybe the next day, during the break between lunch and supper when we were at the gym, I was sometimes able to negotiate a deal where fights didn't happen because of my personal relationship with some of the Fall River people.

There were times that fights did happen, and sometimes I played a role in setting somebody up or getting somebody that we saw as being a real mean-spirited, racist motherfucker. A couple of times I arranged for someone that was ratting to the officers to be dealt with—to get beat up or slapped around.

In the life of being a drug dealer, having girlfriends was part of the mix. Donna was one of the young women I had on the side. When I went to prison, she wrote me letters on a regular basis. Visitors signed in on the table in the office where the mail was. One Sunday when Susan was signing in to visit me, she happened to look across the table, saw a letter for me that wasn't her handwriting, and pocketed it. When I saw her, I didn't know what she was reading, but I saw this look on her face of anger and sadness at the same time. She said, "This is a letter from one of your girlfriends." We had a short argument and she left. Thinking I was going to make things better by being honest. I wrote her a letter that night that basically said, "You're my main person. These are the women I'm just using for this and for that," and "That's the life I live and you have to understand" and I even put in a little poem that went something like "One is my treasure, one is my treat…." The mentality that I had about relationships was so off base that I thought that what I wrote made sense. After reading my letter, where I became even more upfront about what had been going on, Susan said, "That's it. I can't deal with this relationship no more."

She didn't see me for a month or two and then just Sundays she would come with the kids. I went through my changes about hearing stories about her seeing other people. But by the time I got out of jail in 1980, we had pretty well went through the whole process of being angry at each other and getting to a point where we became friends.

I got my GED when I was in jail. You went to class a couple of times a week; it wasn't a real in-depth process, but it did allow me to escape my reality for the moment. Instead of being stuck in a place where you're behind the walls and not doing anything, it gave me something positive to do with my time.

Back then they had the furlough system that allowed prisoners who had good behavior and most of their time served to leave the institution for set hours. I definitely saw the benefit the furlough system had for the institution in controlling people's behavior, because that's one of the things that they held over people's heads. People would be close to a furlough, and if they weren't the ideal prisoner, the furlough would be taken away from them.

At nine months, I got my first furlough. While the sense of freedom of being out was exhilarating, the whole time I had a sense of sadness because I knew I had to go back in there. It was a traumatic experience not only for the inmate, but also for their family members because they also had to go through the experience of having their loved one home and then say goodbye to them again knowing they're going back into prison. During our time together on that first eight-hour furlough, Donna completely lost it a couple of hours before it was time for me to go back. The trauma of having me in prison for that long and then come out and only be out for a certain number of hours brought out some deep sadness in her.

The second furlough was twelve hours, and then the month before I was released, I got a twenty-four-hour furlough. The third furlough was the one where I could spend the night out—sleeping in a bed for the night and waking up in the morning, and being in that fantasy of "Well, I'm out of prison now," and then having to go back in. Those furloughs definitely kept me in check, and I probably was less of a rule breaker toward the end of my time in jail, because I was both looking forward to the twenty-four-hour furlough, but more importantly my parole date was coming up.

9

G's Machine

When I got out of prison in March 1980, I had feelings of culture shock similar to what friends who came back from Vietnam had. Some things on the outside had changed. More importantly, my perception of the community, because living within the prison system is so confining, so concentrated, and everything is so heightened, and now I was out in the real world, so to speak, the limits were not as clear and my life was not so controlled as when I was in jail, but yet I was so sensitive to control that I started to see it all around me. It wasn't like prison walls, but I saw that my immediate environment, my neighborhood was, at some level, a limitation to me. I saw the limits on a financial level because I had been a drug dealer for all those years and that was the only way I felt I could survive.

On the one hand, I was thinking about I don't want to go back in there. Fresh in my mind was the first night in prison. So when I came out, I didn't initially contemplate dealing again for fear of going back into jail. But I didn't know what else I could do.

I felt lost, because my jail term didn't prepare me for anything. Basically what I did behind prison walls was entertain myself. I continued with my dealing in there and trying to find ways to maneuver around the system. It just kept me in the same mind frame. So when I came out, the greatest pull was to do what I had done before going in. Because as long as I was out there dealing drugs for most of the seventies and getting arrested only twice, I knew I could be successful at it. Jail didn't rehabilitate me in any way. It only gave me more time to think about being careful so I wouldn't get arrested this time.

Because I never had dealt with my own self-hatred and issues about my childhood, I continued using drugs. When I first got out, I was mainly drinking and smoking reefer. I still wasn't shooting drugs or doing heroin, but the thoughts were still there.

A good friend helped me get a job working at a residential program out in the countryside with up to twenty-something kids. It wasn't big money by anybody's standards, but especially by my standards because I was used to having big money in my pocket all the time or the resources to make that money.

I became frustrated with my living conditions and, not having the money, the tug toward going back to what I was good at became so great that I started to sell reefer again. I knew a young kid who was making a lot of money, and I started to get a few bags of cocaine from him to sell. Within three or four months of getting out of prison, I was back dealing and left the job.

When I got back into dealing, I had all those years of experience and I eventually started dealing more than this kid could handle and convinced him to introduce me to his supplier. I had this vision of becoming this major dealer again, but I thought I would do it different this time. I was going to create *Gerald's machine* and it was going to make a lot more money than I had ever made before.

I went out and met this Black guy from New York. New York had passed a law where if you had over a certain amount of dope or if you had got busted the second time for being what they called a major distributor, they would give you life in prison. So a lot of the drug dealers at his level left the state of New York and set up camp in New Jersey or Connecticut.

I met him at his house, a nice house out in Elizabeth, New Jersey. He was fronting me I forget how many ounces of dope and how many ounces of coke. I had a couple thousand, but he gave me five times what I had to buy. He brought me back into his bedroom, went into his closet, and came out with a shotgun pointed at me. He said, "I'm giving you this stuff, but I want you to understand that this ain't no game. If you ever screw me, I'm going to come looking for you."

I had a rule at that point that I would never hold. In other words, I would not deal to a street-level user, nor would I ever carry more than a certain amount of drugs on me. Within a six-month period, I grew to a level where I had about five people dealing for me in the New Bedford area. Eventually I had people dealing for me in Boston and then in Washington, DC, where I knew people from New Bedford.

I had no partners, but I had people who worked for me. In each of the three areas, I had one person who was my main contact and then through that contact, we would have several street-level dealers. I had an older brother who was my main person in New Bedford. In the apartment building where he lived, I rented a small room on the top floor where I kept my supplies.

I was making lots of money and putting it right back into buying more supplies. I always got more than what I paid for. I spent most of my time traveling to New Jersey to cop and then back to New Bedford to rest up and party. I had started snorting heroin and cocaine again. I would take the Night Owl, the eleven o'clock train out of Providence to DC. I very seldom flew. Traveling by train was easier in terms of security.

10

Living Dead

Addiction being a progressive disease, toward the end of 1980 my drug use went from maybe four bags a day to fifteen bags to twenty bags a day. I used to snort all the time. I could be in restaurants, clubs—wherever I was I always had stuff on me.

Because I snorted so much, a lot of the residue would get caught in my nasal passages. Eventually I was using so much I never gave it a chance to drain down. In the Maryland hotel where I stayed when I was out in DC, I woke up sick, went to go snort, and couldn't. Nothing could get up my nose because it had seized because of so much stuff in it. The woman I traveled with was an IV drug user. When she woke up and was preparing her *wake-up* shot, I said, "Hook me up." She said, "What are you talking about?" "I'm sick and I've got to get the dope in me. Prepare me a shot." "Gerald, don't do it. Don't stick a needle in your arm, because you'll never be the same, you'll never be able to stop." I had this cocky, brash attitude about it and said, "You're talking to me. I can do this." She said, "No, I'm not going to do it."

As we were talking, a friend who was one of my contacts out there came to the hotel to get his package and take it to another part of town to deal. He was an IV drug user and he had no problem when I said, "Well, since she won't do it, can you hook me up?" That was the first time I shot heroin. I felt a rush come over me almost immediately, while with snorting, it takes a couple of minutes before it gets into your system. If I was to describe it to somebody who never shot drugs, it begins like a warm feeling that started at the head like someone dripping wet honey over me that went all the way down to my toes, and at the same time I felt that physically, emotionally it was a feeling of euphoria. I was like "Damn, this is fantastic!"

Right after I did that first shot, I wanted another. But this time I wanted to do what they called *speedball*, when you mix cocaine and heroin together and inject it. That feeling was probably equal to the first time I had sex. When you have sex the first time, it is such a new wonderful experience. I think every time you have sex after that you're trying to catch that moment and maybe make it even better. The mixture of the two drugs was so powerful that I immediately had him hook me up another shot. The progression of the disease of addiction had reached the injecting drug user stage in me. Snorting drugs would never satisfy my addiction again.

I couldn't shoot drugs myself in the early stages. I couldn't put that needle in my vein right, so other people would do it for me. Because my veins weren't easy to see, it was hard to find places to inject on my body. I used to use my legs sometimes, which would leave them so sore that at times I had to be carried around the hotel room until I got enough drugs to kill the pain. Eventually I learned how to use certain areas on my hands to inject the drugs myself. Once I learned that, I went fast from being a drug dealer to just being a hard-core addict.

In a six-month period, I went from having a growing business, where I was always on the move to eventually all I wanted to do was sit home and shoot drugs—primarily speedball. I spent more and more time in New Bedford just getting high. I gave more and more responsibility of picking up drugs and transporting it to other people, so I lost control—what they call, *lost my edge*. Eventually I was using more than I was selling and I lost everything. I went from having lots of money and lots of drugs to practically no money and a big habit. I ended up getting to the point where I couldn't even go and buy my drugs from Gene anymore because I owed him money. I got word he was looking for me; he was going to come down and kill me because I owed him thousands of dollars from the last few times I had went up there to cop from him.

Three, four 'o clock in the morning I'd be copping drugs out on the street, because when I was chasing the cocaine, it was never enough. You never have enough. I would do my forty dollars worth, whatever it was, over an hour, hour-and-a-half period, and then I went out and, if I had money, bought more. If I didn't have money, I'd figure a way to hustle to get money. When I think about that period, it was the saddest, loneliest time of my life.

People in support groups or therapists dealing with a substance abuser say a *trigger* is something that reminds you of your drug period or entices you into thinking about using again. One of the triggers for me now that helps me to realize how lonely and sad and destitute I was during that period is the foghorns that I hear at night. I can remember being out there late at night, copping, standing in line, hustling, and hearing those foghorns. When I'd be out there and I'd hear that sound, it always brought me back to reality to some degree. Like I'd be caught up into the moment of whatever I was doing, looking for that person I was copping from, and at the same time worrying about the cops pulling up. There was something about that haunting sound that touched something way deep inside of me that said, "This is fucked up."

Even now, years later, when I hear the foghorns at night, it does the same thing to me; it always makes me stop what I'm doing and listen, and a profound sense of sadness comes over me. At first, it's just sadness, and then the memories start to come, and I remember how bad it was. And I feel bad. I feel bad for myself and I also feel bad because I know that right at that moment, as I'm listening to that foghorn, there are people who are going through the same thing. They're out there lonely, hungry, or dope sick—though I've been away from that lifestyle for over ten years, it never fails. Sometimes late at night I sit out on the back porch and hear the foghorns and I go right back to those places. It starts coming right back; it's a reminder of what it was like and it's a reminder of why I'm doing this work: fighting for more treatment and against the root causes of addiction. It serves a dual purpose.

I used to think about the movie *The Living Dead*, where they had scenes of corpses that got up out of the grave and walked. When the foghorns went off late at night, whoever was out there primarily were drug users. We were walking dead. In my mind, we were out there using until we were going to die. We were stuck in this fate of being drug users, of being scum, and it was just a matter of time before we were going to OD, get killed, end up in jail, get infected with AIDS.

No one likes to be out there hooked on drugs. There might be times when you're high and you're not thinking about it, but I think most addicts, throughout their day, throughout their life, they get feelings of "This sucks." But they don't see any way out.

Sometimes when a lit match goes out, the sulfur smell flashes me right back to shooting heroin, because we used matches to cook drugs to liquefy it. Just the smell of it is a trigger, reminds me of that period, and makes my stomach turn. Sometimes the smell of Scotch tape, which we used to tape the bag of dope shut, is a trigger. Not in a sense of wanting to use, but a connection to that time, being out there living in that underground subculture. It becomes a reinforcement for me that says two things: I don't ever want to be back in that place again, and it also reminds me of the suffering that's going on, that there are people who are out there now still sick and suffering.

My mother was one if she didn't hear from you, she would pick up the phone and try to contact you. She would say, "I can always tell when there's something wrong because you don't call," putting the pressure on in her way. I tell people addiction is based in denial and fueled by isolation. My mother would try to fight through that isolation. She didn't want you to feel like you were alone. She always said, "I support my kids no matter what they do. I don't like what they do sometimes, but I support them, I'll be there for them." And she walked the walk. Her door was always open. There were times I used to go to sleep on the couch; she would always make sure I had something to eat. But she never gave me money. This was her brand of tough love.

Eventually, because of the fear factor of Gene, I went to DC. I continued using drugs while I was out there—primarily cocaine. I was trying to do a geography cure and it didn't work. I brought a couple of women out there from New Bedford to become strippers. The effect I've had on some women's lives is something I have to live with. It's not a good feeling at all.

One day I was standing on Fourteenth Street in front of a strip joint while Donna went to get paid. It was the middle of the day, there were hundreds of people walking up and down the street, and the police vamped on me. For a Black man, this is not an unusual experience. This cop walked up to me and, while he was talking to me, he was tapping me with his nightstick. Eventually he heard the little .25 automatic I used to carry, threw me against the car, and took the gun. I was going to do some time, so I left DC.

Things didn't work out well for me back in New Bedford, so I went out to DC a second time. I stayed out there for a while, came back to New Bedford, tried my hand at dealing again and was nowhere near successful. I would make enough money where I didn't have to go out and commit any crimes, so to speak. I could sustain myself by dealing or hustling. My partner at the time worked as a prostitute, so we survived off of that to a degree.

But my habit became so big that low level of dealing just wasn't making it. So in '83, I started doing armed robberies almost every day. Becoming familiar with firearms in the armed forces, being a dealer for those many years and always having pistols around, and some of my Panther history included understanding the use of firearms and having them around us—I fell back on that as a means to getting money.

Fearing that I was going to get myself killed, people who cared about me said, "You've got to get out of here and you've got to get straight!" They got together some money to buy me a plane ticket to send me to northern California. I moved in with my good friend Paul, who lived with his brother, an insurance agent, in a Concord suburb. Being away from New Bedford had some positive effects on me. I stopped doing heroin and cocaine almost immediately, but was still smoking reefer and drinking.

My buddy got me a job working for an agency that had several group homes. My first day they sent me to work at a house for adolescents who had severe emotional trauma and were considered high risk in terms of acting out violently. The next step for them would be to put them in a lock-down institution. Some of them had already been in some kind of juvenile detention. This program was small and more concentrated on teaching the kids life skills all the way from brushing their teeth, taking showers, ironing their clothes, to developing study skills. It used less punitive methods than most other programs.

On my first day, because they had lost a lot of staff people, the staff left me alone in the house with the kids to go attend a two- or three-hour emergency meeting. When they came back, all the kids were laid back. Even though the job was new for me, I was able to use some of my life skills to deal with them. Brought up in a large family, I knew how to maneuver my way through all of the different personalities, where you had to respond differently to each person.

The supervisor told the agency head that he wanted to keep me at the program, because I had a way of working with the kids where I was able to maintain them. Because of the feedback I got from him and seeing how other people who were trained weren't able to deal with the kids as well as I could, I felt a sense that I could accomplish things, that I had something that was of value. That was another brief period of my life where I felt good for a little while. I looked forward to going to work every day. I was one of the only Black staff members. I knew some of the other staff people were jealous—Who is this guy that comes in here, doesn't have a college degree, how come the kids are more looking forward to seeing him than they are me? How come I can't deal with them?

Eventually Donna and Jamaal, my youngest son at the time, moved out there, and my friend's house where we were staying wasn't big enough. We moved in with an aunt, my mother's sister, who lived in Oakland, California. A guy from the East coast who had married into the family was also staying at the house. Willy and I became fast friends.

Though I had this job and felt a sense of worth, I still hadn't dealt with my addiction. One day I came home from work and went upstairs to my bedroom. Willy was the only one home. I smelled that familiar smell of dope being cooked. I knocked on his door and he asked, "Who is it?" "It's me." When I went in, he had the spoon and was cooking up his dope. There was the needle and there were the drugs. "You get high?" He said, "Yeah, I been getting high for a long time." I asked, "Where do you get your dope from?" One thing led to another and the next paycheck I got I went with him to San Francisco, where he bought his dope.

He would take me to this rundown project, where, at night, police helicopters with searchlights would fly over. We used to get high in a shooting gallery run by a guy called The Gypsy. When we got high at his house, we seldom had our own set of works, so we used to use the works that were there at the house.

I was a weekend warrior. Once a week, maybe twice over the weekend Willy and I would jump in the car, go out there and get high, then go back to Oakland and hang out. Eventually I started to use more and more drugs and it wasn't long before I was using full-time again. I was getting high during the week, whenever I could get it. We were supposed to be staying at my aunt's house to save money so we could get our own apartment. Well, I wasn't saving money anymore because I was using it to get high.

On a weekend around midnight, the head of the agency called me up at my job and said, "I need to talk to you as soon as possible." I told him, "Well, I can see you Monday." "No, I'll come over right now and talk to you." I hung up the phone and thought I know what it is, they found out about my getting busted in DC for having a gun on me, he's going to come over here with the police and they're going to arrest me. I went over the edge. I took all the money they had, took their van, and went to find Donna back at my aunt's house, bought a plane ticket, and I was out of there.

I found out later that one of the kids had accused me of beating him up, because I had used restraint on him, like you were supposed to do in certain situations. His parents had some kind of political influence and were going to press charges against the agency. The agency head wanted to come over immediately to get to the bottom of it, because he was fearful of what was going to happen. I could have explained it to him without any problem.

Back in New Bedford, I took up what I was doing before. I had a little better handle on my addiction, so I was able to pick up a little bit of drugs and sell and sustain myself. I had a family member who had become big in the cocaine trade in the city. Even if I got behind, all I had to do was go to her and she would help me back out, so I never had to go without.

11

Hitting Bottom

In the spring of 1984, I started to get one ailment after another. I didn't know what was going on. My health was just going down. I eventually went to the community health center where a friend, Kim Holland Pope, was my doctor. She is a Black woman who I was in the Panthers with and went on to become a doctor. She was one of the people who got shot during the July 1970 incident when Lester Lima got killed while I was out in Germany.

During the summer of 1984, she started questioning why I was getting sick so often. At my brother's wedding in August, I was so sick I almost passed out and had to go back home. I went to the health center the following Monday. Dr. Pope told me I had hepatitis and mononucleosis at the same time.

It was September when she said, "You know, I'm really concerned where your health is at, and I think there's something significantly wrong with you. Looking at your blood count and other things, I think that you either have some type of a cancer that we haven't figured out or you have that new disease called AIDS." They started testing me for the cancer and she sent me up to see Jerome Groopman at the Deaconness Hospital in Boston. He was one of the country's leading doctors in AIDS research.

At the same time, Donna was pregnant with my second son with her. It was going to be my first child I was going to see born and I was her birthing coach. I was still getting high, shooting up, through all this period. We were sort of together but at the same time, as in most of my life, I feared intimacy and commitment to one woman and was always in more than one relationship.

The end of October 1984 I experienced the two extremes of life, dealing with birth and death. I was in the delivery room and saw my son Jewel enter into the world. Being there to see a woman having a child and that child being mine was a spiritual moment, one of the most profound experiences in my life. When he was coming out of his mother's body into this world, I was like, "Damn! Women are awesome." I was empathetic toward her because of the pain she was going through, but at the same time I was excited and happy about seeing this child born. Here was Jewel Marcel Ribeiro lying there, healthy, bright-eyed.

Sometime later, whether a few hours or a few days I'm not sure, the health center called me and said that Dr. Pope wanted to see me. As I sat there in the examining room and waited, I had an uneasy feeling that I was about to hear bad news. At the same time, I was still all pumped up about seeing my child born. When Dr. Pope came in and I saw the look on her face, I was petrified. She just came right out and said it, "Gerald, I don't have good news for you. Dr. Groopman called to tell me you have AIDS." I was like, "What?" She told me, "You have ARC, AIDS Related Complex, and you have about a year and a half to live." Anything that followed, how long I stood in the room, did I get up and walk around, what she said after that, I don't remember.

What I do remember is feeling a sense of hopelessness so deep and so profound that it encapsulated everything that had felt negative about me, all of those negative things I had experienced and felt on the inside—the person who was devalued, the person who had this fate that said that nothing good was supposed to happen for him—all those things hit me so hard that it was like putting an exclamation point on all those feelings. Worthless! Devalued! It was like she was saying to me that everything I ever felt or heard negative about me was right. That's not what she said and that's not what she meant, because we were friends and she cared about me. But that's what the diagnosis meant to me.

When I left the health center, I had two reasons to go drink. Because my culture taught me, you have a baby and you go have a drink because you're happy. And when someone tells you you're going to die, you go and drink because you feel sorrow.

I immediately told my family, whereas nowadays many people won't tell anybody. We had a family culture where we were taught to support each other. If one fights and you are there, you better be fighting too. Don't come home and say, "I saw my brother fighting" and didn't jump in. So it was easy for me to tell them that I had AIDS.

That night my brothers, sisters, and I all spent the night together over my sister's house—drinking, crying, laughing. It was like a wake/party all at once. It was that family support that got me through where I didn't commit suicide, because the feelings were just too strong. Within one brief span, I had seen my son born and then was told I was going to die—you can't get any more extreme than that.

I went into a complete downward spiral where my addiction totally took over. I didn't care about anything at that point. My get-high partner, my hustle partner, was Maria. When we had apartments, they didn't have any furniture. The only thing we had was a mattress, maybe a little black-and-white TV, a kitchen table, a frying pan that we did everything with, a couple of cups. It was the barest of barest necessities. Those were the only things we had in the apartment, because the only time we used it was to do our drugs and to crash.

We survived on bologna sandwiches. Sometimes that was the only meal I would have in a day. Sometimes that was the only food I would eat over a week, sometimes longer. We used to go to a meat market in Weld Square, where you could get sandwiches real cheap and buy enough sandwiches to last for a couple of meals. Bologna sandwich would be our breakfast and it would be our supper. I still love bologna; it is like comfort food to me.

And relationship-wise, you don't have any relationships other than with the person you might be hustling with. Everybody else is someone that you're trying to figure out how you can use, or people that you're trying to stay away from because they want to hurt you because of what you did in the past, or family members who care about you but you don't want to be around them because you know you're going to hear the right thing and you don't want to hear it at that point. The craving for the drugs is what controls everything. It's eat, sleep, and get high.

Heroin is a drug that you need a wake-up—a *wake-up* meaning when you wake up in the morning, you need to get high the first thing you do in order to function, because you wake up sick. Morning doesn't necessarily mean a.m. Morning means when you entered into the next day, whatever time of day that could be. Heroin and cocaine is a bad mix because you wake up in the morning and don't have your money for your wake-up, because when you're a cocaine user, you use your money chasing your next shot of coke until there's no more money left.

This was a period when my addiction was totally controlling me. I wasn't dealing, just surviving by my wits on the street, along with my partner. She did what a lot of women who are addicts do, I hustled people. Sometimes I pretended to be a cop and hustled prostitutes or their men. I used to pull up on them like I was a police officer and take their money. I don't know how they didn't know that I was just another addict, but I played it off. I also used to sell *beat bags* to the out-of-towners—people from Acushnet, Dartmouth, Freetown, the Cape, fishermen, people who didn't know me or didn't remember me, or probably knew me but didn't know me as an addict. Beat bags were just milk sugar or flour. We would *beat* them, in other words—take their money and go buy dope with it.

But my primary thing was robberies. More than once I came close to being killed. One night when I was on a rampage, I borrowed a pistol from somebody I knew. I didn't know if the pistol worked; all I knew was I was planning on using it like I normally did, just to scare people to get what I wanted to take care of my addiction. We planned to hit a liquor store and parked two blocks away, around the corner. While the person I was with sat in the car waiting, I walked into the store and said, "This is a stickup!" to the person behind the counter. Just as I was pulling out the pistol and pointing it at the person, I saw movement out of the corner of my eye. Another man came out of a walk-in freezer or back room and was reaching for something I realized was a pistol. As he took aim at me, I pointed my pistol toward him and pulled the trigger. The gun didn't work. Everything stood still for a moment. He ducked and then came back up. But by then, I was flying out the door. From that point on, he didn't have a good shot at me. I ran all the way to the car and we got away. We went and did a couple of other places before the night was over.

Our house was a traditional shooting gallery. Because we lived down toward the Weld Square area, third-floor apartment, small street, and because we knew a lot of the people out on the street, because we grew up with them or because I dealt with them, a lot of them who copped in that area would come right to our house to get high so they didn't have to leave the area. When you get high at a shooting gallery, whoever's house that is, you give them some of your drugs. That's how it works. So that was another little hustle for us for a little while.

But you never have enough money because you never have enough drugs. So we went from one apartment to another because we always got evicted. We didn't pay our rent: forget the rent, we needed to get high. Forget eating, I needed to get high.

Eventually we ended up homeless, never slept out on the street, always found a way of staying over so-and-so's house. We ended up staying over a family member of Maria's in Westlawn projects for over a year. She was an addict and her house was a shooting gallery. The craziness that went on over there was unbelievable, all the way from people overdosing, having to carry them out of the house, putting them on the lawn someplace, and then calling the ambulance or the cops to come pick them up, to people kicking the door in because they knew someone who had just beat them was in the house, to sleeping and waking up and finding somebody going through your belongings. I was HIV positive, still sharing of needles went on, as it does today. I knew I was living with this virus that was supposed to take me out. Hopelessness turned to just plain not caring.

Remembering that period, I say today that when you talk of people being dis-enfranchised, you can't get any more underclass than being of color, poor, home-less, addicted, and living with a terminal disease with the stigma that AIDS has. Until we begin to get people from that level involved with the struggle for social change, there will be no true social change. They are of the barest of feelings. They're right there feeling the pain of life—that's what they're living. So the peo-ple that come from that place where they're so low on the spectrum of this capi-talist society, I think have much value to bring to where I believe humanity is going, to the next level.

I can add to the discussion about oppression and social change or dealing with the drug problem or the AIDS issue, because I can talk about it from experience as opposed to just, say, understanding from a book or empathy. Even though I may not have a formal education, I have the experience of knowing what it feels like to be in that place and what it feels like to be able to come out of that place—the causes for people to be in that place, the work that it takes to come out of that place, and the barriers that you have to overcome—and to come from that place is what drives me.

That's why I know that when we start to talk about Gerald the community person in terms of people's perception of who I am and the perception that I have of myself and how I defined myself before I was able to do this work, I know the bottom line is that I am no different than any of the people who are still out there in terms of what's inside of me. There's nothing special about this person. What seems special about me to people is the experience that I'm able to bring to the table. And because they don't hear it from people, or they don't hear it enough, it sounds unique and it sounds like this person's different, but it's not. For example, the recovering people involved with our outreach work have great potential in terms of being able to add to social change work. I see that in them and it excites me to no end. On the other hand, because of my impatience—and my impa-tience comes from my understanding of the pain that's out there—I get frus-trated because I know what they can add, but I also understand that growth will happen when people are ready. Not based on my timetable.

12

Trying to Get Recovery

"Just Say No" might work for someone who's not using drugs, never used them, and is in a situation where they're not likely to. But for people who are at risk because of the social, political, and economic forces that have control over you, you just get blown like grass in the wind. "Just Say No" doesn't have any meaning to them at all. Because first of all, no one really says "yes" to this whole life anyway. I never said, "Yes, I want to stick needles in my arm, put myself at risk for getting diseases, and live on bologna sandwiches." It was a process that got me there. And it took a process to get me out of there. And "Just Say No" is definitely not a process. It's a slogan. Rhetoric does not solve social problems.

What triggered my getting into treatment was the old cliché that's used in AA [Alcoholics Anonymous] and NA [Narcotics Anonymous]: I was sick and tired of being sick and tired. The holiday period of '87 was my last serious run in regard to the illegal activity around supporting my habit. I was dope sick and went with two Black women down toward the Cape to bounce some checks. We would buy stuff with bad checks, sell it on the street, and then use the money to buy our drugs. On the way down, the trunk popped open and we stopped on the highway to close it. We got back in the car, took off, and were riding for another minute or two when an unmarked police car pulled in front, another pulled in back, and then all of a sudden the flashing lights, and they pulled us over. They searched the car, didn't find anything that was illegal and were getting ready to let us go, then decided to take us the Bourne State Police barracks to question us and do a body search. When they did a computer search and found out that I had warrants on me, they kept me there.

I was there from Friday evening until Monday morning. It was one of the most horrific times I've spent in my life. They gave me a thin wool blanket, same blankets that they would give you in the armed forces. I had it thrown over the top of my head and wrapped around me like a parka, and I was sick. I paced and every time they walked by the cell to do the check they saw me pacing. I must have looked like a caged animal to them. Every time they walked by me, I would stare in their eyes with so much contempt. They would say something like, "Hey, how you doing?" and I would grunt toward them. You weren't supposed to have anything to read in there, but one guy came by and said, "Here, you want something to read?" and gave me a newspaper. Another guy came by and said, "Hey, I ordered a couple of sandwiches and I only want one. Here." He gave me one of his sandwiches.

Those three nights, Friday, Saturday and Sunday, were hell. Those days I came as close as I ever have to going insane. I was in a cell in a secluded area, so I didn't see anything, didn't hear anything, I was just there. It was just my thoughts and me. That was my bottom in terms of saying I can't live like this anymore.

Monday morning they took me to Wareham District Court. I spent the whole day in lockup in District Court. At the end of the day, the Dartmouth State Police came and picked me up because I had warrants on me in that district of the court system. I spent from four to nine o'clock that night in the Dartmouth station in their lockup. Then the New Bedford Police came and picked me up, because I had warrants in New Bedford. At the New Bedford Police station, they put bail on me and my mother and father came and bailed me out. When we got outside the door, I said thank you and went my way.

My way was I had to get straight. I was sick as a dog. That weekend was a time of reflection on how much pain I was in. Not knowing where it came from, but just knowing that they had told me a few years before that I was going to die from this disease, and here I was still living and basically had done nothing with my life but get high, hadn't dealt with the issue of my disease of HIV/AIDS. It was at that point that I considered trying to change my life around—try and get away from the pain of drug addiction.

I got on methadone a short time, but got kicked off because of cocaine use. Although the methadone was dealing with the heroin, the counseling and its effect on me were minimal. Leaving the program, I told my counselor, "You people see me as a nail, and you think the only way to deal with me is with your power, like a hammer, and I think you deal with everybody in the same way." Though I was still active and didn't utilize my ability to critically think things out, I felt the oppression, the control, the lack of individuality in the program. When I was on methadone, I felt like I hadn't dealt with my the addiction in the way I've left it today, where I've become empowered and have, to a large degree, been able to deal with the root causes of my addiction and continue to deal with those issues on a daily basis. I got recovery in spite of methadone, not because of it.

People need to understand the difference between detox and drug treatment, because people think detox is drug treatment. Detox deals with the physical effects of the drug on the body and the neglect that, by being on drugs, you do to yourself—like you're malnourished from not eating. Most people go into the methadone program as a detox client and then begin thinking about how can I get on the maintenance program, and that's like digging yourself into a deeper hole. Getting off methadone the two times that I did—the first time getting kicked off, then getting back on, and the second time getting off a little bit slower, were among the most painful experiences of my life. For people who don't understand what it feels like, think about what it feels like to have the flu and multiply that times ten. Methadone is like mental handcuffs that become physical handcuffs when you don't use it, because the pain is much more intense than the detox off of heroin.

That reality is used as a tool to keep people in the methadone program. Many more people could get off the program if they were given the opportunity to look at ways to do that. To begin with, you should have a therapist who fosters that type of thinking from when you initially go into the program.

Methadone has been used to control the vast majority of people who are on it, as opposed to helping them to take that step into not just abstinence from illegal drugs, but recovery—to recover not only in terms of the substance abuse issue, but also the abuse they might have experienced as a child, their neglect by society, their lack of hope, and all the other root causes why people choose to self-medicate. Like why are they depressed in the first place? If we didn't have a society that is based on denying people their basic needs and creates this sense of hopelessness, it would be much easier for me to support a program that utilizes methadone to help people. That's why we need to look at the much broader picture rather than blaming a person for being an addict and saying let's keep him on methadone so he won't go out and create more harm in the community.

At a national conference, I met a man who ran an inpatient drug treatment facility in South Carolina. This program used methadone for the detox and when the person went into the rehab, they began to wean him off of the methadone. Some people might need to be on methadone in their rehab for a couple of weeks and some might need to be on it for longer.

The word *maintenance* never came up in my discussion with him. Methadone was used to ease the withdrawal and to help the person begin to get some order to their life, but all within a structured environment. The object was that the person would leave there and their aftercare would not include waking up every morning and going to get methadone. The goal always was for the person to become drug free and empowered to deal with the issues that were the underlying causes of their addiction. If people were given another philosophy about their addiction, about their life in general, and if opportunities were created for people in the way that they should be, you wouldn't have twelve hundred people in New Bedford lining up every day to get their dose of methadone.

13

Getting to the Here and Now

I had been to a couple of drug treatment programs, and I basically went to them because of the court to show I was trying to do the right thing. But when I was truly sick and tired of being out there and trying to get recovery, I didn't have a clue what it meant. The closest I could come to describing what recovery meant was "Oh, just stop using drugs."

I had no concept of what addiction was in terms of how people get into that position, how it takes away so many things in your life, the amount of energy it would take to get recovery, different processes you go through in terms of understanding when you make these quantitative changes over days and weeks, and then you make these qualitative changes over a larger period of time that just happen because of experiences of maybe relapsing, going to meetings or counseling sessions, or experiencing something of life that you haven't done while you were active, but it reminded you of times before you were self-medicating. And it doesn't necessarily have to be a happy thing, it could be even a sad thing; you're experiencing these feelings and they let you know that you're alive. Even if it's a sad moment, you realize that it doesn't come anywhere near how bad it is when you're using.

Many times when I was at a bad place, Susan would take me in. Not sleeping in the same bed as husband and wife, but like brother and sister. She never turned me away.

She had graduated from college and become an engineer. We had been separated for a few years, but because we were still legally married, she got me into a twenty-eight-day drug treatment program on her health insurance. There was detox plus the rehab. It was at this program that I first heard the concept that addiction is a treatable disease. That to me was the beginning of my recovery process. I realized that it was not my fate to always be an addict. So there was an understanding, on the barest level, that there was something I could do about it. I didn't know what that was, other than the program was based on the twelve-step NA model.

Now programs, for the most part, people go three or four days. You can't even detox in three or four days. So when people look at that and say treatment doesn't work, they don't understand that that's not really treating people.

It comes down to programs that have a real good structure, are long-term, and deal with the person holistically—the mental, emotional, physical, vocational, relational, and spiritual aspects of that person. Programs that deal with all of these dimensions will be more successful in helping an individual than programs that are short-term and deal with just one or two aspects of the person. It's important that an individual be ready and willing to put the work into it. But if the program doesn't look at the person in a more critical way of how this person got to be in this position where they need help, and then help them deal with all those issues, it's not likely to be successful.

In the beginning of my recovery process, I talked with my counselor about the fact that I had never resolved my baby brother's death and never talked to anybody about having felt responsible. When my parents came up for a family session, I talked about his death as being one of the main reasons why I had so much self-hatred. My mother explained, "Your brother didn't die from falling off the table. He had water on the brain and wasn't expected to live a full life." She helped me to understand that I needed to let go of that—which the adult in me wanted to believe, but the child deep down inside me thought she was saying to protect me. Through that process, I think my mother began to understand what addiction is and how I ended up using. She realized that it had emotional roots, while before she saw it in religious terms of breaking God's laws.

In my treatment program, most of the groups that we attended were workshops with a specific task or topic. You worked on one of the steps or they talked to you about the physical effects of drugs on your system, relapse prevention, or other aspects of being an addict. But they had a one-hour period every day and the only thing they would say at the beginning of the hour was, "Okay, these are the rules. We don't want to talk about war stories. We want to talk about what's going on right here right now."

So we would sit there and people would look around the room and maybe some small talk would be going on. If someone started to speak about something that happened to them, the counselors would say, "You can't talk about that right now." Or if someone started to say, "When I get out of here, I'm worried about—" "You have to stay in the here and now."

We all used to hate that hour. I couldn't figure out what we were supposed to do during this time. I felt totally frustrated, frustrated beyond words. So frustrated that it became a powerful feeling that took control of me. I started talking about how frustrated I was sitting there and not knowing what we were supposed to be doing. Other people started chiming in. On probably the fourth day, people started talking about how they were feeling and it dawned on me, I know what the purpose of this is: it's to get us to know what we're feeling. So we were feeling angry or afraid, happy or sad, but it was about keeping things in the here and now.

That is a key tool that I use today. It's important to not let yourself be controlled by your feelings, especially when you're not in touch with them, because that could lead you to relapse and could keep you in a position where you can't grow. Your feelings are actually supposed to enhance your life, to complement the rational part of yourself, not control your life. Not to run away from your fears, not to be so happy that you become manic and not know why, and not become so depressed that you get caught in that place, but to try to stay in the here and now and know that sometimes when you're acting out angry at somebody, it's not actually about what's going on right at the moment. When you figure out where the emotions are coming from at that moment, you start to realize that it's about something else.

Recovery involves more than being abstinent. *Abstinence* means just what it says: you abstain from something. If you're a recovering addict who's abstinent, it means that you're abstaining from your drug of choice and other drugs that bring harm to you.

Recovery is looking at the different aspects of your life, what makes you who you are, dealing with all the different issues that made you self-medicate, and trying to get better in all aspects of your life: building relationships with your kids, your family, your friends, your community, your higher power. Recovery is an ongoing process, not a place that you get to and say, "I've got recovery and therefore I got it all together." It's a lifelong process in which you're always challenging yourself, you're always trying to get better, you're always giving back, you're always trying to relate to your fellow man the way you want to be treated.

The word *recovery* shouldn't be used just in the context of addiction. When I tell my story, I say I'm a person in recovery—someone who's not only recovering from substance abuse, but recovering in a much broader sense. I'm recovering from racism, classism, sexism, homophobia, all the different "isms" that divide and oppress people. To achieve recovery, you have to tackle the issues of disenfranchisement because of the color of your skin, the class that you come from, your gender.

For the first several months of my recovery process, I was totally immersed in going to different groups: I went to NA programs, one-on-one counseling, family counseling, and an HIV support group. I remember walking into my first NA meeting and getting a newcomer's pin and then getting the thirty-day drug free pin.

Then I used cocaine. When people said that I should go up there and get another newcomer's pin, I asked, "Why?" "Because you picked up, so now you've got to start over." That didn't make sense to me. Because the way I understood it, recovery was a process and part of the recovery process was there was a good chance that you were going to have some relapse. Relapses were not something that you could say were a negative or a positive, but they were part of the nature of the beast in terms of dealing with your addiction. So I didn't go get another newcomer's pin. But I kept coming.

From that time, I never totally bought into NA. It helps people to abstain from drug use and in some ways begin to recover their life. But for me, there was too much emphasis put on the abstinence piece and on me as an individual as opposed to me being part of a community. The way NA plays itself out in a lot of people is to limit their involvement in the community and not enable them to grow to some degree. Those support groups can put people in another type of denial where they don't face some of the key issues they need to deal with, both internally in their own life and externally in terms of dealing with what's out there that affects them, such as racism, poverty, classism, sexism—all of the issues that make up the *fabric of oppression.*

In a perfect society where you don't have people going back to depressed, hopeless neighborhoods and situations, recovery would be much easier to achieve. So it creates a causal effect in terms of people using, but it also becomes a barrier for someone who gets into a treatment program and wants to recover in terms of gaining back some self-esteem and some purpose in life, getting a job to feed their family, and all that.

When I was on methadone and lived on Ruth Street, I faced an uphill struggle, because here I lived right in the middle of a drug-infested area and I had to walk through those streets to get on the bus, go get my methadone downtown, get back on the bus and come home, and all along the way back and forth, when I made that walk, I passed all the people I got high with and all the people I dealt with. And then I'd go back to the same house with no job, really no understanding of, socially, how I ended up in this position, no skills in terms of being able to get out of that situation.

More than a couple of times, I thought, well, I'm in recovery now, so I can deal drugs again. As soon as I'd get the drugs, and I might have it for a day, but the whole time I had it, it's talking to me. "Well, you got seven bags; you only need to sell six in order to re-up, and you can probably sell them six today, so that's fine." And I'd end up using.

It's a miracle that I was able to succeed when I look back at it. I used to get my check from the VA [Veterans Administration] on the first of the month, and before the first week went by, I used to be broke, because I would pick up. I would stay clean for most of the month, and as soon as I got that check, I would pay the rent and then I'd last for a couple of days, and sooner or later, one of those walks, either up or down, I'd end up giving into that craving. One bag—oh, one bag ain't gonna hurt. Before I knew it the money's gone and I wondered how was I going to make it through the rest of the month. And I'd make the same mistake over and over again.

I really, really wanted to get away from the drugs. I understood that I was not in a place where I could hold onto my monthly VA check. I told my mother where the check was sent, because I had moved all over the place, and explained to her my dilemma. So she started holding my money for me. I sat down and told her all my different tricks, I even showed her where I would get high, so there were times I might go there and tell her, "I need money for such-and-such," and she could look at my hands, because this is where I used to get high, and see if I was using. I explained to her what my face and my behaviors would be, and this way she could say no. "You need food? Sit down, I'll make you a plate." "You need such-and-such? Well, your father will take you to go and get it." That worked for me—me being totally honest with her and her holding the money and playing the gatekeeper role, not forever, but there was that period where I needed that extra support early on in my process of recovery.

I can't give it all to luck or all to the spiritual realm. Even when we're the sickest of sickest in terms of whatever disease we're dealing with, we still have that will, that ability to make choices. In a lot of ways, my job now is to help people see that they have that will within them and to focus on that as a source of strength. When I sit down with someone who wants to stop using drugs, what I'm trying to do, when you break it down, is to give them the understanding that they have choices. And that choice means that they need to will something to happen, which means they have to put the work into it. Whether they're on the street, whether they're in a program, whether they have relapsed in their recovery, whether they don't have a job, you still can do something about your situation.

I decided to go back to school. I had some time under my belt now. I was still in recovery, but I was not abstinent, because I still would do a bag or two from time to time, still touching the flame now and then. I was still growing. I continued to look around me, and the old feelings were starting to come back in terms of seeing myself in the larger context of things as a poor person of color in this country. I was thinking, I remember the riots and when drugs really started to pour into the community, and I saw myself before I did drugs, when I was dealing drugs, when I became an addict—all these things would come into my mind and I started to understand that I needed to do more than just stay away from drugs.

I enrolled at the local community college for the spring semester of '88. I had a Volkswagen that took me back and forth to school. I started staying at Susan's house, because I wanted to put myself in a better environment than Ruth Street.

In terms of all the times I've been in school, that one semester was the best. Even the tough subject for me, math, which I never did well in at school, I struggled at the beginning and then started to grasp the concepts, and it was like a light went on and I just took off with it and got a B+.

But the two classes that I excelled in were Writing from Experience and Sociology. Learning to me is picking up something and being able to apply it in some way to my own life. I loved sociology, because it fed into everything that had been previous to getting into the drug trade—my feelings back around the riots in New Bedford, when I was in the service, when I was in the Panthers, my concept of why I was going to stay when the Panthers left and I wanted to create this change. So that part of me started to get massaged and come to life.

When I consider the word *grace*, Professor Rachel Holland (whose daughter I was in the Panthers with and later was my doctor) and Reverend Chavier are two people I knew personally who had grace. They both seemed to enjoy a sense of inner peace, to possess wisdom, and have an ability to nurture themselves and the people around them. Both of them gave me a sense of my value, of hope for a better future. Professor Holland would tell me, "Gerald, you have a gift for writing. You should take that and do something with it. You should write a book on the riots in New Bedford because that was really a microvision of what was going on across the country."

I made the Dean's List. But during the summer break, I lost my focus and didn't go back to school in the fall. I definitely had the support at that point, but

I didn't have it in me to go every day, because I was still using cocaine and heroin. As they say, you can't serve two masters.

Working for the Governor's Office for Vietnam Era Veterans, my brother Jack had a big space at the old vocational high school. He said, "Why don't I give you a little space and you can begin to write your book here." At the library, I researched the history of New Bedford and the Cape Verdeans. I interviewed community people like Manny Costa and Jack Custodio relating to that period of time before the riots and trying to get an understanding of what were the preconditions that set up the riots to happen the way they did in New Bedford.

I needed other things to do with my time, so Jack said, "You can volunteer to help with the Thanksgiving Day and the Christmas baskets for the veterans." The work around collecting the baskets was therapeutic. It was also my introduction back into doing community work.

Jack set two guiding principles: "Always be on time for your meetings. When you tell people you're going to be someplace, be there. And when you take on a task, make sure you follow through. That's going to give you credibility." Those two simple rules have served me well, especially early on when I first started doing the work, when people knew I was a drug addict and all the negative connotations that brings up. But when I was always on time and followed through with my responsibilities, I gained the reputation as someone who took what I did seriously and who people could depend on. I always tell people who begin to work with me, "If you take yourself and your job seriously, you will do those two things." Some get it right off, while others struggle with it.

When Thanksgiving and Christmas were over and we were entering the new year, Jack told me there was a woman, Liz D., who was doing HIV prevention work in the community. "I know they're having a meeting at the Verdean Vets. Maybe you should go if you want to find something else to do with your time." At my first meeting of the Community Working Group on AIDS Education, they were talking about what outreach they would do that summer. That summer of '89 we passed out HIV prevention flyers at the Memorial Day parade, the Verdean Vets parade, the Fourth of July, and other community festivals. People said outreach work seemed to come natural to me. I started to redefine who I was and get clear about what I wanted to do.

14

Rebirth

In August of '89, the Community Working Group on AIDS Education set their sights on doing a conference entitled "Empowering Our Community: New Bedford Responds to the AIDS Epidemic." We asked Reverend Graylan Ellis-Hagler, pastor of the Church of the United Community in Roxbury, to be a keynote speaker. He talked about substance abuse in a way that most people hadn't heard at that point—how communities of color were the primary targets of the government's War on Drugs, how what was going on in Black neighborhoods was basically the same thing that was happening in South America, how the criminal justice system was warehousing people of color.

Recovering people associated with Reverend Ellis-Hagler's church had founded the Treatment on Demand Coalition that May. We met with Moses Saunders, who was key in forming the Coalition. We asked the Coalition to present a workshop on people in recovery doing street outreach to addicts to prevent the spread of HIV—because two-thirds of New Bedford people living with AIDS contracted the virus from blood-to-blood contact through IV needle sharing.

But in order for street outreach to be successful, treatment needed to be available when and where an addict needed it. Liz D., Leo B.—who like me was a recovering addict who had HIV—and I decided to hold a pre-Election Day rally in New Bedford to raise the issue that there weren't enough drug treatment programs. One thing I got from Liz was basic grassroots organizing skills, which she had learned in North Carolina from Black women involved in the civil rights movement. She was very methodical in her approach in terms of there's a task and a step-by-step process to accomplish it.

Organizing the rally helped me to come out of the closet, so to speak. It helped me to look at that part of my life when I was active in my addiction as not necessarily a negative, but a positive. It helped me to understand that because of these experiences I had something to add to the discussion about drug abuse in the community.

A couple of days before the rally, I sat down with a newspaper reporter to tell her about the rally and about what it was like to be an addict. It was the first time I came out in a public way to tell people, "Hi, I'm Gerald Ribeiro, and I'm a Black man, a son, a father, a community member, an addict in recovery, and an organizer." It helped me to put my stuff out there—they say you're as sick as the secrets that you keep. The first sentence in the article was "Gerald Ribeiro spent six weeks pumping heroin into his veins as he waited for a drug treatment program." And within it, I talked about my bottom, the fact that I was now in recovery, the fact that I understood that I was dealing with a disease that I could arrest and the root causes of my addiction.

Most importantly, it talked about the lack of drug treatment programs. We should deal with addicts not as bad people, but rather as people who have made choices that create harm to themselves and the community, we shouldn't just lock them up, there's not enough help for them. My message was different and they gave it a prominent place in the newspaper. They were using it for their own reasons; it sensationalized the drug abuse issue, it made people want to buy the paper, but it also served our purpose, because it brought people to the rally.

Being an election year, many of the city politicians came out. The focus of the rally was the lack of drug treatment and that, in order to change things, we had to get involved with the political process. Near the end of the program, we had people line up—most of them in recovery—and go over to City Hall to register to vote.

The rally was one of the highlights of my early recovery process. Previous to organizing the rally, I was basically educating people about how you can prevent yourself from getting AIDS. Now I was out there calling for a policy change: "You people need to make sure there's more programs for us." It brought me to a degree back to my roots in the Panther Party.

Treatment on Demand now has a rule that to become an outreach worker, you have to be abstinent for a year. I had six months, and here I was a co-founder of an organization that was dealing with recovery issues and playing a public role in informing other people—not only people who are in recovery or dealing with the virus, but also people who react to those issues. It was a transformational process for me. In the first months of Treatment on Demand, a lot of the work and thinking about what our next step would be fell primarily on me because both Liz and Leo had full-time jobs.

We didn't know where we were going with Treatment on Demand as an organizing concept in New Bedford, other than we wanted to keep up this public awareness campaign letting people know there's not enough drug treatment programs, and we've got to do something about that. We circulated a rough flyer inviting people to an organizational meeting scheduled right after an NA meeting, because we were thinking that the big recovery community in New Bedford was the pocket of people that we were going to pull from to build this organization. The room had about thirty people in it, but only five people stayed. I couldn't understand—why is everybody leaving? This is about trying to help other addicts.

On the other hand, I was excited because two of the people who stayed were Richard C., who was in recovery for only a short amount of time, and his wife, Sharon. He said, "Well, I'm looking for something to do" and was at the office that following Monday.

In that initial stage, Treatment on Demand was about people in recovery calling on other people in recovery to become advocates for a community-based continuum of care from detox to aftercare. We spent a lot of time just trying to explain to people who we were, because a lot of people, even well-meaning people, were turned off by our name, Treatment on Demand. "Maybe you should change your name to Treatment on Request or Addiction is a Disease Coalition, something like that." We would look at the question and, whether we had a five-minute or an hour discussion, it always ended up that Treatment on Demand made a statement, and the statement was that we were no longer going to see ourselves as victims, that someone had to wait six to seven weeks to get into treatment was a problem, and that we had power and we were going to do something about it.

When a young cousin, Keith Ribeiro, got shot on the street, the community got together and planned a march to signal our concerns for youth. After the march, we established the Youth Action Committee to address the lack of positive things for kids to do. While the younger kids did arts and crafts at the weekly meetings, the older kids planned dances, trips, and other events.

Around the same time, the Racial Justice Coalition was formed when three Black men who had a cleaning business had been stopped and brutalized by the Dartmouth Police and the State Police. As co-chair for that, I helped put together a racial justice conference. I also got elected to the Board of the Greater New Bedford Community Health Center, which my mother helped to found to provide health services for low-income people.

When early in my recovery I started doing work in the community, there was no one happier than my mother. When I got an award from the Massachusetts AIDS Action Committee, she went up to the event in Boston even though she wasn't feeling well. Shortly before she died she came to our AIDS Awareness Day event and spent the whole day there in the sun. She told me that she wasn't feeling good that day, but she wanted to be there; she wanted to support my work not just in words but also in deed. A couple of days later she went in the hospital and a month later she died.

When the area anti-poverty agency gave me their first annual community service award, I made a qualitative leap in understanding what I was about. In presenting the award, my friend Debra R. said, "Gerald has been working on many issues to help people in this community." When I went up to receive the award, I responded, "I am not a man who's dealing with many different issues. I'm dealing with one issue—oppression." And if that was the case, then I had to choose my struggles wisely. If I was spreading myself thin, I wouldn't be able to focus and do what I needed to do from the bottom up. Understanding that the lowest you can get in society was to be a Black, addicted, poor, HIV positive person, I decided Treatment on Demand was where I needed to put most of my time and energy.

That night I chose to let go of some of my other commitments. Leaving the Youth Action Committee was the most painful. When it originally started, like most things, everybody wanted to help out, but over a period of time people started to trickle away and it ended up falling apart.

15

Power Shared

At the end of 1990, Treatment on Demand decided to incorporate and formed a board of directors, with me as staff person. They paid me a $25 monthly stipend, but with money coming in because I was a disabled vet, I could afford to work full-time for the organization. This was critical for our early success.

In structuring our work, we looked at five areas of focus or what we called the *five keys* to unlock the doors for more drug treatment: increasing public awareness, getting the community involved, registering and educating voters, holding government officials accountable for their decisions, and obtaining government funds for treatment programs.

To broaden support for drug treatment, we put a lot of time and energy into building a statewide base—getting chapters up and running in Fall River and Springfield. But statewide organizing took too much from our limited resources. In time, we decided to pull back our state organizing committee and restructure the organization to focus primarily on building a local model for community empowerment.

I was involved in forming the board of directors and deciding how the board should function, but not fully understanding what that meant for me. In building an organization for social change, we wanted to put into practice that whole idealistic thought about how society should be—that power is power shared. I had to go through a mental shift in terms of giving up some of the power, some of the decision-making on what path we would take. I had come from the street mentality of being in control of things that I developed. When I was dealing for those many years, I was always the person in charge or part of the nucleus of the crew. I made decisions about how things were going to go or what we were going to get and how much money we were going to spend and who was going to do the deal.

As the organization grew, I had to go through a let-go process, giving up some of the control and feeling a sense of loss. I was being pushed, not so much by other people, but by the process and vision that I helped to set in motion. When you have so much at stake in building an organization, when you were there when it was born and you're there as it's growing, and you're taking a major piece of it in terms of the work and the sweat, letting go is not an easy thing to do. I compare it to watching my youngest daughter grow up and seeing her go off to college, and seeing her thoughts being shaped by other people. I had to get to a place where I understood that somebody else might come up with another way of doing something that was just as effective, maybe more effective, than my own. I had to put faith in the group, just as I had to have faith in my daughter. People in the organization had to get to that same place, because I put myself in that position where people depended on me to make the decisions and do most everything.

There were times when I had to come back to the group and say, "You were right and I was wrong." My pride was never so big where I couldn't come back and say, "I've changed my mind." If someone said, "Wasn't it you who said such-and-such a couple of months ago?" I would answer, "Yes, that was me. But I got new information that changed my mind." In change work, pride is something you have to put in check.

To get more treatment, we had to create a community consciousness around the issue of substance abuse, to get people to understand addicts and addiction in a less reactionary way, because addicts were primarily vilified. In community awareness marches and rallies, our literature, our cable TV shows, conferences, presentations to religious and civic groups, coalition-building with other organizations, and voter education campaigns, we personalized the issue of addiction, where people were able to put a face to a name.

In staff training and street outreach, we made the issue much bigger than saying your problem is substance abuse and you should keep abstinent from drug use, and that's the beginning and the end to it. We talked about the need to focus on the demand side instead of the supply side. We said people become addicts because of the negative situations and circumstances they find themselves in. How a person responds to those situations in many cases is to self-medicate with some mind-altering substance. We said addicts should no longer allow themselves to be targets of attacks aimed at denying the dignity, humanity, and rights of people who use drugs. We educated the public about the role that recovering addicts could play in dealing with the issue of drug abuse at the community level.

Through this process, people started to see that addiction was a community disease, that there were root causes, that it affected people in the community at all different levels, whether you were using or not using; when an individual lost control of his reality, they then lost the ability to dream about what they could do in the future. And that was parallel with what happened in communities: when communities lost control of their reality, their environment, they would lose the ability to envision a better community.

What Treatment on Demand did was peel back the layers of the onion by asking the question "Why?" Why is the War on Drugs directed towards certain communities when drugs are used throughout society? Why do people use drugs in the first place? Why is the government not using proven strategies to stop a disease that's killing people? Along with encouraging people to ask questions, the other role that Treatment on Demand played was to say, "Okay, now we know why this is happening to us. Now let's figure out how we can work together to do something about it."

Based on our understanding that poverty and oppression fuel the drug abuse and AIDS epidemics, we broadened our scope of work to include issues that put the rights and health of people first. If recovering people just went back to their devastated neighborhoods and had no skills to get a decent job, treatment programs were just going to be revolving doors. If people can't find affordable housing and health care, they are going to get swept up by that culture of despair where people can't see a future. If kids live in a polluted environment, how are they going to thrive? If most people in the county jail are there for drug-related crimes, why aren't they being offered treatment? If prisoners need to build up their self-esteem to succeed in the outside world, why are we going to humiliate them and their families by going back to chain gangs? We saw that all these issues were pieces of the same puzzle.

As we broadened our mission, we expanded the makeup of the board. While initially the board was primarily people in recovery, we started to bring in people from the faith community, people who worked on affordable housing, children's issues, against U.S. policy in Latin America. Many were white, middle-class. When these community activists who I had known from their work joined Treatment on Demand, I got to know them on a more personal level. As I got to know their history, I saw there was a common thread in all of us—an incident or circumstance happened when we were young. The experience left its mark on us, which helped develop our empathy and connect us with efforts to bring about change. I'm not talking about the typical social service volunteer, but rather those folks who see working for social change as integral to their lives. Some may have a job that has nothing to do with changing things at any level. But their driving force is trying to help humanity by challenging policies that oppress people. They may have a job, but this is their work. Allying with these folks gave us a wealth of skills and experience that we used to further the mission of Treatment on Demand.

I worked with the expanded board to tap new funding streams and put together a mixed, more stable funding base. We got government programs to pay for our HIV prevention work, while grants from progressive-minded foundations supported our community organizing work.

In 1993, when we did our first strategic planning process, my level of burnout was evident. We said we need to sit down and look at what is Treatment on Demand doing right now and who's doing it. After we listed everything that we were doing, we saw that I was working on most of them. When we looked around the room and saw fifteen, sixteen people, when one person was doing three-quarters of the work, it was clear that there was a major problem here—people couldn't only be involved with the decision-making, but also had to participate in the work that needed to be done and have the commitment level to make sure it got done.

Getting people to start doing more of the work was difficult. But eventually we reached a place where decisions were being made and work was being done that I had nothing or very little to do with. That wasn't something that I could envision in the very beginnings of Treatment on Demand. It was difficult for me to miss certain meetings and events because of health reasons. I thought that I had to be there, no matter how I was feeling. Now I'm able to say, I can't do this, I can't do that. We as an organization got past the feeling that if I'm not there, the world's going to fall apart. If I'm there, it's going to work one way; and if I'm not there, it can only work out different. Sometimes I can make the case that if I was there, things would have turned out better in the short run. But, realistically, there's no way I can be everywhere I want to be.

The first time I felt that sense of loss of control was like hitting a speed bump without any warning. At first, not even knowing what it was, and then identifying it, and then being able to say, "Okay, here comes one of those times again," seeing it before it comes, to the point now where now I look forward to those times.

16

Yes or No

My early work with elected officials began in 1989 with my brother Jack, who was an advocate for veterans' issues. Based on his connection with the mayor and a couple of the city councilors, I was able to meet them and develop my own relationships with them. From being out on the street and dealing with many different personalities and situations, including life-and-death situations, I learned skills that helped me work with politicians—how to listen, how to read their body language, how to negotiate with them, how to sort through the rhetoric, how to posture myself, and, in some situations, befriend them. That being said, I found most of them to be complex individuals on the surface but very predictable on the level of what drives them.

One of the most difficult lessons I had to learn was to not personalize the dislike I had for them and the positions they took on issues that were near and dear to my heart. At times I did personalize to the point where it crippled my ability to reason how to best move our agenda along. Like the county sheriff and his opposition to needle exchange, his efforts to revive chain gangs, and other stands he's taken I see on a personal level as being evil, I feel like I could never come to terms with him. But I know that I have to conduct myself in a way where he cannot push my buttons where I allow my emotions to take control of my actions and thus alienate myself.

In the summer of 1994, we asked the City Council president to speak at our annual AIDS Awareness Day event, because we typically had a local official come, present a proclamation, and say a couple of words about the city's commitment to AIDS prevention. He wasn't responding, so I said I would talk to him. "This is an issue that's facing your constituency and you should be speaking on the issue," I said to him on the phone. He told me he couldn't commit to it. I could tell that he was basically sidestepping, not knowing how to say no to me. He didn't return my calls.

I saw him at a Hands Across the River march dealing with environmental hazards of PCB contamination of the Acushnet River and the harbor. I walked alongside him and picked up where we left off on the phone that day. Again he said, "I can't," and we went back and forth, back and forth, and I could see that he was getting frustrated. How dare I challenge him? I kept hammering away, hammering away, and finally he looked at me and said, "To tell you the truth, Gerald, this is an issue of priorities and AIDS and substance abuse are not a priority for me." I looked at him, feeling full of rage, and the first thought that came to my mind, I wanted to hit this guy. Then I said to myself you can't deal with these folks that way. Tears welled up in my eyes as I walked away from him. When the rally was over, I must have had the meanest look on my face and at the same time the saddest heart.

I called another city councilor, a man of color, to present the proclamation on that day. He said yes, but it was conditional: wait until after the city elections before you talk about needle exchange to local elected officials. At the time, we were just launching our needle exchange campaign. I thought about all the people I knew who had died from AIDS, all those who were infected, and the many more who were at risk of becoming infected. And here we had two city officials who were basically telling me that we were disposable human beings. I thought, we can't just allow this lack of concern to happen without responding in a way that held them accountable.

I get great pleasure thinking and coming up with a creative way of accomplishing what we need to get done, whether it's developing a name for something or steps in an organizing campaign. Like a lot of my most creative thoughts, it came to me late at night when I was alone: we should create a format where these politicians had to respond to people's concerns before elections. No pre-election debates had been scheduled at that point. If we could sit down and work with the neighborhood Crime Watch groups, we could co-sponsor ward debates and each ask the questions that were important to us, schedule one debate for candidates running for the at-large seats on the City Council, and hold a mayoral debate.

Up to this point, the neighborhood Crime Watch groups were seen by us as part of the problem, because they had come together as a basically reactionary force in response to drug abuse and crime in their neighborhoods, and here we are talking, "Well, there wouldn't be so much crime in your neighborhood if people weren't addicts, and there wouldn't be so many addicts if there were jobs. And the jobs wouldn't be cut back the way they are if capitalism wasn't set up the way it is." As we at Treatment on Demand were looking at all the issues, I said, "Wait a minute. These neighborhood groups are a plus along with the fact that they're already organizing. The problem is, from our perspective, they aren't really addressing the root causes of the issue, but at least they aren't people so filled with apathy that they aren't doing anything." I didn't agree with what they were doing, but at least they were coming together and organizing. Thinking about us as being bridge builders, I saw that these neighborhood groups were what I call *non-traditional natural allies.* We viewed ourselves on opposite sides of the fence, but in reality we had the same goal in mind: we wanted a better community. I realized that, in the bigger picture, people would have to come together from many different ideologies and reasons why they got involved with this struggle for us to have what we would call real social change.

There was some resistance to my idea even among Treatment on Demand board members, thinking that it was too idealistic or setting our sights too high. "You're talking about organizing eight debates. It's too big a task to pull off in a few weeks." My response was you use the energy that's out there. Treatment on Demand can pool its resources with the Crime Watch groups, maybe even look for a couple of other groups, like youth groups, anybody that's out there organized, and bring them into this coalition. People asked, "What's the purpose? The candidates are going to soft-shoe around the issues." I said, "They'll only answer the questions if we control the structure of the debates, and we tell them that in order to answer the question they have to say 'yes' or 'no' and then why."

People didn't think that the Crime Watch groups would go for it. But I had already started to build a relationship with some of the people in the neighborhood groups because we were both part of a citywide drug abuse prevention effort. Before meeting with the Crime Watch groups, I did my homework in thinking this step out. I like to put myself in other people's shoes and think of potential questions they might ask me so that I am prepared. At first, people were somewhat hesitant about me even being at their Crime Watch meeting, because I'm supporting needle exchange and treatment for addicts.

I needed to appeal to people's self-interest. By finding the commonalities between you and them, you make them more sensitive to your concerns. If someone says to me, "I'm against this because I'm sick of addicts breaking in my door," I take in what they say, and then I'm coming back with, "I agree with you, lots of crime in this community is related to addiction. But the methods we've been using aren't working. Another approach in dealing with addicts on the street is to get them into a drug treatment program. And don't you know there is no detox in New Bedford?" People would respond, "No?" or "What is a detox?" Then I would explain what it is and why it is important. I said, "I don't want my father getting whacked upside the head by somebody trying to support their habit. So I support having police to protect him. I'm just for a more balanced way of dealing with this problem, where there is equal emphasis on treatment, enforcement and prevention and not put all the resources into enforcement."

I continued, "Do you know that there aren't going to be any pre-election debates this year? Basically, people are going to be voting on name recognition, and you might be voting for somebody that don't—what do you want, foot patrol? You could potentially be voting for somebody who doesn't think foot patrol is a priority. Wouldn't you want to know where they stand on certain issues before you help put them in office?" The group took a vote and said they'd work with us.

First called the Debate Committee, it took on the name *CIVIC*, the acronym for *Citizens Informing Voters In the Community*. In the debates, each organization got to ask three or four questions that related to their issue. We put out a report card on how candidates stood on the different issues. We also videotaped the debates and aired them on local cable TV.

The debates were non-partisan; in other words, we weren't out there supporting one of the political parties or any candidates. What we were supporting was getting clear answers to questions that related to the community. The candidates were uncomfortable about that. But they couldn't say no, because they wouldn't be saying no to just Treatment on Demand. That was part of the strategy. It would have been easy for them to say no to this fringe group of recovering addicts and people who supported them, liberal, but much harder for them to say that to the middle-America Crime Watch groups. Much harder for them to say that to this broad coalition that represented different sectors of the community. True to our philosophy of being bridge builders, we reached out over the years to other advocacy groups that represented other interests, like the elderly, young people, anti-poverty groups, and small business organizations.

CIVIC educates people about the importance of educating themselves, about organizing, about electoral politics and the limits of electoral politics in the context of living within an economic structure that controls what the politics are. Through voter education initiatives like CIVIC, people move from voter apathy to what I call *voter reality*—they come to understand that you can only go so far through the electoral process. Only by pushing those limits can we create a more democratic society. CIVIC is one of the most important cornerstones of what we try to do on the local level, not because it's going to change the politics so much as it's going to change how people perceive power, how they can influence power, and how they can begin to become power themselves and see that they have the power to bring about change to a more just society.

17

Stayin' Alive

One issue near and dear to my heart has been needle exchange. When Mike A., a person in recovery, came to a Treatment on Demand meeting in 1990 to promote needle exchange, we were initially resistant. Here we are talking about treatment and getting people off drugs, and this guy is talking about giving out needles?

But we saw several reasons to look beyond our first reactions and investigate the issue: first, knowing that sharing needles was the main way people got AIDS in New Bedford. Secondly, addicts would continue needle sharing due to the state's antiquated drug paraphernalia laws; Massachusetts is one of only four states in the country where it's still illegal to buy a sterile syringe without a prescription.[11]

We also understood that addiction is a progressive disease; not all addicts have hit bottom and are prepared to stop injecting drugs. Or they may want to stop but can't get into a drug treatment program and continue using drugs during the wait period. Some like me, early in my recovery process, didn't have the wherewithal to remain abstinent. Relapse is a strong possibility when you keep people in that same setting that made them addicts in the first place. If needle exchange was a way we can stop people from sharing potentially infected needles and getting a disease that's going to kill them, then we needed to support it.

Bill S. and I attended a conference on needle exchange in Seattle and found out that needle exchange was working in other American cities and other countries. The research showed that by reducing needle sharing, needle exchange programs slow the spread of AIDS without increasing drug use. Where needle exchange programs operated, there were fewer discarded needles in the streets and parks, because addicts traded the now valuable used needles in for new sterile ones. When we came back with this information, the statewide Treatment on Demand board decided that we were going to support it.

That was when we adopted what's called the *harm reduction* approach, where you reach people at the level where they're at and help them to take any step to reduce the harm they're doing to themselves or to others. You accept that some addicts are not ready for treatment and focus on reducing the negative effects of their drug use. For an addict on the street, first steps might be better vein care—not shooting drugs in the same vein all the time—or preventing abscesses by using alcohol to clean your injection site before you shoot. Another step would be to use new or bleached needles to avoid abscesses and possible exposure to HIV. Over time you try to get active addicts to consider and then enter drug treatment. Because of the nature of drug abuse and the fragile recovery process, you have to respond to the high rate of relapse in a non-judgmental way, keeping the focus on supporting people in using clean needles or other harm reduction techniques as they move back and forth between active addiction and recovery.[12]

Our support of needle exchange marked the beginning of total separation between us and the Boston chapter of Treatment on Demand and its founder and leader, Moses Saunders. Moses' mentor was Reverend Ellis-Hagler, who was running for Mayor in Boston. Though he was running against a popular incumbent, Reverend Ellis-Hagler had a good following in the Black community.

Needle exchange was being done underground in Boston at the time, but not in the Black community. John P., who was part of an AIDS advocacy group, decided to set up shop in Dorchester and Roxbury without educating the people in that community about the benefits of needle exchange. They immediately got turned off to needle exchange on an emotional level and, to a degree, a factual and historical level, but with no critical analysis of needle exchange itself. Here comes the white man again with another form of genocide against our community. People equated needle exchange with the infamous Tuskegee experiments, where Black men were left untreated for syphilis. Seeing people up in arms over needle exchange, Reverend Ellis-Hagler took up the fight against it and got people behind him in his run for political office.

At the same time we released a statement to the newspapers saying that we supported needle exchange, Moses, being under the wing of Reverend Ellis-Hagler, came out in Boston papers saying that he was against needle exchange. The media called and asked, "What's the confusion? Are you guys for it or against it?" So we called Moses and told him, "You can't do that. You can't take a stand that says you're against it when we decided, as a collective, that this was the best thing for us." But the campaign in Boston for Mayor was in full swing, and that's when communication broke down between Boston Treatment on Demand and us.

In other countries, needle exchange is seen as an emergency health care measure. But in this country, we have to contend with the politics of needle exchange, explaining what addiction is and getting people to understand that we're all interconnected, and what happens in this underground subculture affects society as a whole, and how politicians use addicts as a way to stir up voter anger and deflect attention from the problems that fuel addiction. In our campaign for a city-based needle exchange program, we looked at different sectors of the community, saw how they looked at the issue and what role they could play, and brought them on board in a thought-out way to form the Coalition to Protect Our Families—like a little wave that builds into a big wave.

We slanted the argument in different ways to different people according to their ideologies and self-interests. I appealed to the faith community, "You know, Christ says to reach out to those who are the weakest, the least among us." Folks understood that; we had major support from the religious community. I explained to people involved in Crime Watch groups that needle exchange was cost-effective; it was cheaper to provide clean syringes to an addict while trying to get them into drug treatment than it was to pay out $150,000 to treat someone who had the virus.

To reach the politicians, we did everything from phone banking to setting up educational sessions for them, to taking them on field trips to see needle exchange programs, to bringing in people who ran programs and out-of-town law enforcement people who supported needle exchange. But the most powerful way to reach the politicians and give them the political will to support needle exchange was getting enough of their constituents to let them know that they wanted it in their community.

In July 1996, the City Council passed needle exchange nine to two. Though there was local support out in the community for needle exchange, we understood that there were powerful forces working against a city-based program. The Mayor, the District Attorney, and other opponents got a referendum question on the ballot and mounted a campaign of fear and misinformation about this proven harm reduction method. In the November election, the City Council-approved needle exchange program lost by a two-to-one margin.

Though we took that defeat hard, I tried not to lose sight of the victories—that we registered hundreds of new voters and persuaded thousands of voters to support the needle exchange plan, when only a few years before there was almost no community consciousness about what addiction is. Organizing for needle exchange, people saw that what they were fighting against was political—a group of politicians who cooked up mistruth, fear, and hate toward addicts and did not appreciate the value of every human life.

Getting a needle exchange program in New Bedford would have to be done on the state level. I got a commitment from the Department of Public Health Commissioner to convene a meeting of the statewide needle exchange working group to sit down again to come up with a strategy to get needle exchange programs in communities that needed them. At the beginning of the meeting, I gave a ten-minute spiel about the history of the needle exchange struggle in New Bedford and how the local approval requirement needed to be removed from the state legislation establishing needle exchange programs. If there was a tuberculosis outbreak, would you need local approval to implement emergency public health measures that numerous research studies have proven to greatly reduce the rate of infection?

The ensuing conversation was all over the place, with a lot of middle-class service providers in comfortable jobs talking about this in the abstract. I was the only Black person in the room. The way I was coming at it was: this affects *me*, this affects people I know. I am not going to sit here and waste time in a conversation that wasn't heading anywhere in particular. I said that a lot of people accuse me of being impatient and that statement had some truth to it. I'm impatient because I am living with this disease, both in terms of having it in my own system and in my work, seeing people around me dying and family members being devastated.

We can't sit back and keep talking about educating. At some point, you've got to realize it's not education that's the problem. It's opposition from people who lack the political will, or moral will, and plain don't care about certain people dying from this disease. And what are you going to do about that? You have to take yourself out of your direct service mentality and start working for social change.

18

About Political Capital and Me

There's the person that the community knows, there's a person that your friends know, and there's the person that you know. No one knows really what's inside someone else. But the people who know me the best know that even though I do have an ego, I am basically a shy person. I like to have fun, I like to joke, but I'm really not the type of person that likes to be out there. So when I get recognition awards, that's the hard part for me.

I remember when Treatment on Demand first started and I was beginning to feel empowered, I had this pencil—just a regular black pencil, but on the side of it in gold was printed "Black Warrior." I don't know how this pencil ended up in my hand and I never could find another one, but I had it for a long time. This pencil meant so much to me, because whenever I would go speak or I was writing something, that pencil was with me. Because I was nervous about speaking, I used to stare at it sometimes when I was getting ready to get up in front of people to speak. That's what I saw myself as: a Black warrior for social justice. That's how determined I felt in my early days when I was doing this work.

People say, "How can you be a shy person? You deal with the media; you talk in front of people all the time." These are opportunities to put out our message. These are times when you realize the importance of what you have to say and have to shove your ego or lack of to the side.

When I get recognition awards, I look at them as political capital. The fact that *The Standard-Times* selected this Black, ex-convict, AIDS-infested, recovering addict—and all the other negative attributes they might want to put on me—as "Man of the Year" was political capital, not just for me, but for the organization and for everything that we believed in. That shy guy, I put him to the side because it's bigger than him.

Those kinds of recognition, either received in my name or in the name of the organization, I see in a greater sense as here's some more political assets to put in your pocket. Here's some more credibility for you to sock away. Here's a bigger box for you to stand on to speak the truth. Here's a bigger piece of paper to write, with a bigger pen so more people can see it. This is about you and Treatment on Demand having a louder voice now to convince more people, to wake up more people, to get more people involved with this wave of humanity working for social change.

But the one my family gave me on March 2, 1997 was definitely about me and for me. The plaque inscription read: *"For living up to your destiny, as a true soldier in the struggle for social justice."* When I got over the shock of walking into a club full of family and friends, I felt like I was a Black Cape Verdean warrior for social justice.

There were two other ones that held a lot of personal meaning. One was from the Elks Home, the place I grew up around, grew up in, drank in, sold drugs in, went back there to do a presentation and they surprised me by giving me an award. When they gave me the Manny Costa award, that was another one like the village coming out and saluting me, "Well done. Keep doing the work that you're doing."

I can say that it has been a legacy given over to me by my mother and people before her, a legacy that is firmly planted in the survival of Cape Verdeans on those barren islands, the legacy of Martin Luther King, Malcolm X, and Ivory Perry.[13] That's my compass, and north would definitely be my feeling for humanity.[14]

19

Teach the Children

Maria and I got into recovery at about the same time. We were both living with the AIDS virus and didn't see ourselves living a long life. For the first three years of Treatment on Demand, I was in a monogamous relationship with her. Because I was striving to be truthful with myself and with those around me, I felt I owed her something and wasn't about to cheat on her.

When we got into recovery, our daughter, Shanté was around eight years old. Neither of us had spent much time with her. When she was born, she was with Maria for a little while, then she ended up with Maria's parents, then she'd be back with Maria, but there weren't any long stretches of time where she was with either one of us. Maria's sisters and brother had addiction problems too and some of them had kids who were in the same situation that Shanté was, where their parents weren't around most of the time and ended up leaving them with Mrs. Gomes to take care of.

With the number of children in the household and living in the projects, Shanté had to pretty much fend for herself. When we'd go by the house, she would complain to us this happened, that happened. Early in our recovery, we decided it was time to take responsibility for Shanté's upbringing. We went and picked her up under the guise that we were just taking her for the night. The family didn't struggle with us as much as we thought they would when we didn't bring her back. I think, on some level, the grandmother was relieved because it was one less child she had to worry about taking care of.

As far as Shanté coming to live with us, there were some things that we had already set up in our lives. We were living as a "normal" family as much as possible. For instance, we knew we needed to have some discipline around our eating habits and taking care of our personal hygiene. Having our own apartment, having a refrigerator with food in it, that to me was a major accomplishment. Cooking, sitting down to a meal, sitting home and watching TV in the evenings, going to bed at a decent hour—all those things where examples of us creating healthy structure in our lives. I wanted to celebrate that structure. When we were out there living as active addicts, structure was so non-existent that I didn't even wear a watch. Now I was going back to church. I was in counseling and support groups. Acting as parents helped in creating a new image for ourselves, redefining who we were.

Still, it was a big adjustment bringing our daughter into our house. Growing up in a household where there wasn't much limit-setting, she didn't feel the safety that comes with boundaries; she had a lot of trust issues and was full of fear that erupted as anger. We didn't have a lot of knowledge about raising children, though I had some experience with Jonathan and Nsenga when they were very young. So I had some feel for setting limits, teaching her personal hygiene, helping her to view school as being important in her life. Shanté saw that Maria had difficulty enforcing rules and boundaries and would wear her down a lot of times where she couldn't do that as easy with me.

While we were trying to be accountable for Shanté, we were also trying to be there for one another and to keep progressing in our recovery. Maria had a difficult time with this. She would stay away from drugs for a while, but then end up using from time to time. There was a lot of turmoil going on within me. The healthier I got in terms of my emotional self, the more I realized that my relationship with Maria didn't have a solid foundation. The relationship was based on our lifestyle out on the street—selling drugs, doing drugs, and sex. Her continued drug use started to drive a wedge between us, which, for a relationship that didn't have a good foundation, was devastating. It was only that promise of "We're both infected and we're going to die together" that kept us together. I tried my best, but the gap between us widened and eventually our relationship ended. It was difficult to finally let go because I feared I would always be a single parent living the rest of my life alone, dying alone. I believed I probably would never be in a relationship with a woman again because I was poison, infected with a deadly disease that I could transmit to anyone I got close to. But life moved on.

Being a single father of a young girl becoming a young woman was difficult and sometimes scary for both of us. I could be a great dad, but issues that a mother would normally be there to help a girl going through puberty with were tough for us. When an issue came up that was too sensitive for a father to address with his daughter, I sometimes called on a sister or my mother. But mostly I went by instinct.

Although Maria wasn't living with us or there to help bring up Shanté, the house became much more manageable because there wasn't the question of whether somebody's going to be here today or what state of mind are they going to be in and all that. It became easier to raise Shanté because I could set limits and not have to worry whether Maria was going to allow Shanté to do things that she shouldn't do.

Shanté had a lot of animosity toward her mother because her mother would do things like make promises and not come through for her because she had to take care of her habit. Many times when Maria was around or talking to Shanté over the phone, Shanté would curse at her and say, "I hate you." On one hand, I could understand her pain and anger; but, on the other hand, I knew it was wrong for her to be speaking to her mother that way. Maria would sometimes bring herself down to the level of a child, because as they say, once you start using drugs, your development stops. At times, I didn't know where to draw the line.

Whether Shanté was in a loving place or an angry place toward her mother or me, I tried to put it in the perspective of what addiction is, how addiction happens in society, and how addiction happens in a human life. When she was younger and tried to understand addiction and its effect on her mother, I explained it as being a physical sickness that is also an emotional sickness. When she got older, I explained it as a sickness that is caused by social conditions. Shanté probably understands addiction better than a lot of people because of the experiences that she's been put through and the education she got along the way. While she has a good understanding of addiction, she has to deal with the emotional issues when she feels let down by her mother again. She gets hurt and angry and looks to me for guidance, "What do you think, Dad? Do you think she's picked up? What should I do? I told her this is her last chance, and I hate her for what she's doing to me and what she's done."

The second or third year after Maria left, my daughter got me a Mother's Day card and wrote a message about how much she appreciated me always being there for her. I knew then that she had begun to depend on me and to trust me.

Of course, we had to go through the struggles that happen between a parent and a child, including the separation teens need to make to form their own identity. But she and I also understood that we were in this together for the long haul. Going away to college created a lot of anxieties in her, because I think she projected on that separation from home what it would be like to lose me to death. I think it immobilized her for a time where she had difficulty focusing on school. But she was able to work through it and she's going to be the better for it, because she deals with mortality through my mortality all the time. I think it's going to make her more passionate about her life and more open to trying new things.

Being close to Shanté and having an idea of the pain that she's experienced has helped me to better understand my own life. There is a lot of overlap between what we experienced coming up—people putting you in your place, telling you you're not capable. Similar to my own experience, Shanté's schoolteachers were always white, with an upper middle-class mentality. Their value system conflicted with what my daughter was seeing and hearing at home and among her friends and fed into her feelings of self-doubt and self-hatred.

The high school was going to put Shanté in the next to lowest track even though she had done well up to that point. When I challenged their decision, they moved her up two tracks, where she was able to maintain her grades. The school officials said it had been a mistake, but I think it was based on her color and her gender. If I didn't dispute it and they didn't change it, I don't think she would have gone on to college. How many parents from my community had their children put in lower tracks, but didn't feel like they can take on the system? Those kids are probably some of the same kids who are sitting in the House of Correction today.

Young people are again and again painted as the culprits for problems in our society, blamed for where they're at even though they have no real power. A lot of Shanté's childhood friends are dealing with oppression in the way that I dealt with it—by self-medicating. These are kids who I saw growing up laughing with life in their eyes, and now they're at this point where they're being pushed down so much that they see their choices as being one drug or another.

It begins with young people feeling a sense of hopelessness, not feeling love, not feeling any power, and where they look for those things is through sex and relationships that are often unhealthy. Being liked or loved by that young man or young lady becomes easier to attain than the bigger picture of trying to get your education or trying to get ahead in the world. It's much easier to look at your friend and say love is important to me, having a relationship is important to me, having a child is important to me; I have something that I can love that can't walk away from me. I have some control over my life because I have a child. Becoming a teen parent is more a symptom of someone being disempowered than someone saying, "I want to get pregnant because I want to get on welfare." I have never talked to a young woman who ended up getting pregnant who has told me that was the reason why. It always came down to, "Oh, I love him," or "I wanted a child, I wanted to have a baby. I wanted to have something that I can love." When you look at the issue of addiction or the school dropout rate, the root cause is people being disempowered. It all comes down to people being disenfranchised, not having say in their life, feeling like they have no control over their life, and they try to find it in little ways. And all too often those ways end up being self-defeating.

In Treatment on Demand's Youth Empowerment Program, you learn about who you are and where you came from. Look at history and learn that the Constitution was written by rich, landowning, and, in some cases, slave-owning white men to maintain their interests and that there have been people organizing ever since to get their piece of the pie—women, people of color, immigrants.

A teacher once asked me, "What am I to say to young people? They're not going to hear me when I talk about the dangers in life." My answer was, "What would you say to somebody if there was a train coming down the track? Would you soft-stroke it? Would you tell them in a whisper? Or would you scream as loud as your voice could scream, 'There's a train coming! You better get out of the way!' Now whether they want to hear it or not, the facts are there. You don't have to soft-sell it, you don't need to hard-sell it. You need to say the truth: 'Are you going to get run over or are you going to do something to help me take that train off the track?'" As I understand it, the locomotive of that train is the economic system that is based upon exploitation of people—not only in this country, but this community we call earth.

Besides helping young people to understand what it is they're facing, we teach them to take responsibility and take action: "Yes, there are a lot of external factors that make it difficult for us to have some say on what goes on with our life, but you can do something about it." It is teaching young people a different way of looking at themselves, from being completely powerless to having power in themselves and multiplying that power when they link up with others. In our Youth Empowerment Program, young people have produced and aired public-access cable TV shows, organized house parties and done street outreach where they have taught other young people about AIDS prevention, and planned major events that combined information with entertainment.

Relating back to when I was that age and not having positive things to do and just hanging out, I know how easy it is to fall into that bottomless pit. The biggest thing that we can do as adults, as allies to young people, is to help them see there is a way out. It begins with that whole attitude adjustment and seeing where they are, then that process again of re-identifying who they are as a positive person, to have a purpose in life, and then getting that education—not just education in school but education about how the system works—to better equip themselves to get a job, to be a parent, and to contribute to their community.

Shanté has two parents that are living with AIDS. She has seen two aunts die—one from the AIDS virus and one a victim of the unsolved highway murders of eight women supporting their addiction by prostitution. Having experienced so much pain and loss in her life and still trying to move forward, she inspires me sometimes when I'm at my lowest low. Shanté says she wants to do something in the area of advocating for children. Clearly, it's about her own life and what she's experienced. I can see her one day doing that job and doing a good job at it because she will have the empathy and the understanding of what it's like.

As much as I may have done for her, having her in my life did for me also. I missed out a lot with my other four children by not being there to bring them up. I was there for the very early years with my oldest two and even a shorter amount of time with the youngest two boys. Living with and taking care of Shanté allowed me to work out some of my feelings of guilt and self-reproach about past decisions I made.

Shanté sees the private G at home, but she also sees the public G. At one point, her mother and father were seen as scum of the earth. Where I'm at now makes her feel proud and affirms her ability to dream, her ability to have hope no matter what she has experienced. She's one for saying, "You have to allow the past to be the past. You can't forget it, but you can't allow the past to control what you're doing today." That's one of her biggest criticisms with her mother. She thinks her mother is living in the past because of what she experienced and that her mother needs to let go and live today for today.

20

What Has Love Got to Do with It?

Through my recovery process, I started to understand that I didn't know the significance of women's role in my life—or even how human beings relate to one another. My first wife, Susan, was seventeen when we first met; I was nineteen. Though our beginnings were in the progressive movement, I was seeing other women. Maybe it didn't happen as often, especially when we first started to form a relationship, but I always had to have sex with somebody else. I didn't understand the difference between love and sex: love to me was sex and sex to me was love. So that meant that everybody I was having sex with, I loved them to some degree. And if I loved or liked somebody, I had to have sex with them. I couldn't have a relationship with a woman without trying to take it to the level of having sex.

There were periods when I was having sex with several women. It wasn't until I went into therapy and started to understand who I was and what I was about that I started to see women and sex in a different way and realized that up until that point I had never opened myself up and been intimate with anybody—male or female. Intimacy was something that I was afraid of, going back to my relationship with my mother. Because I perceived my mother as having pulled away from me, I was afraid to get close to somebody because they might pull away from me too. Whenever I started getting close to someone, I created a triangle to keep it not real. I didn't ever let it get to the point where I opened myself up and became vulnerable to anybody.

When I started doing community work, I began to treat women differently. Even though I still mainly saw them in a sexual way, I didn't act it out. The first and foremost reason why I didn't allow myself to come on to them was that I didn't want anybody to get my HIV.

When Shelly Perry joined Treatment on Demand in 1992, we worked together on production of our cable TV show. Her empathy and strong sense of what's right and wrong got my attention. One day she said, "Why don't we take some time off and take a ride? I'll take you for lunch." I seldom took a lunch break; once I got to the office, I'd be there way past what would be a normal workday.

When I told her that I was infected with the AIDS virus, it was like somebody had punched her in the face, she broke down and started to cry. The intensity and suddenness of her response touched me. Within two weeks from when we started to be friends, I just opened up to her, like a floodgate, revealing all the pain that I had experienced from childhood through my adult years.

I never thought that I would hook up with somebody whose life experience was so far removed from my background. Shelly is white, HIV negative, sixteen years younger than me, and from a middle-class background. At the same time, we had many things in common. We both love animals and had wanted to be veterinarians. We are strong, passionate, opinionated, brought together by our common commitment to social change.

In time, we said we loved each other and wanted to be together one day. We knew it would be a long process, because we were both in relationships that we had to break off. We got married in 1998. My biggest fear in the relationship has been that somehow Shelly would contract the AIDS virus. We use all of the barriers to make sure that doesn't happen. Whatever the safe-sex guidelines state, we take extra steps.

This was my first intimate relationship. With all that comes with being out in the sun, so to speak, Shelly allowed me to be myself, without the mask, not that public person that always had to be strong.

21

Empathy Disorder

With a lot of people I knew back when I was a dealer and during my active years, the connection now is a limited one both in terms of how often I see them and the quality of the conversations we have. They know and I know that the friendship we once had was based on the lifestyle of using drugs. Even a two-minute conversation with some folks who are still out there is tedious in terms of trying to find things to talk about, because all I want to talk about is why don't you think about stopping using drugs and recovering your life and not live like you're living now; and all they want to talk about is how many women they've screwed over the past year, how much drugs they did, and how good this drug was. It's history, talking war stories, and I have little tolerance for that after a while. Nothing different; they look the same, maybe older. But the conversation is just like if I ran into them four or five years ago. So when I run into them and they're buzzing and they're in that whole mind set, it's hi and bye; if we're in the same place, we might share a couple of sentences more than that, but basically that's it.

There's times when I just want to grab them and smack them and say, "Get a grip! You can do this." I know their kids and I know their kids are missing them. When I get that way, I get uncomfortable with myself, because I don't want to be judgmental. I know what it takes to end up in that situation. I'm not in their shoes; I don't know how difficult it's going to be for them to get recovery. And I know my reaction to some degree is from my own needs: it would make *me* feel better to know they're doing better.

But when I run into them and they're truly looking for help, it's a good feeling because I'm in a position where I can try to help them, where I know everybody who's using needs help in order to get away from it. You can't do it on your own.

My mother could pick up on where people were at, see through the mask and see what was going on. One thing my mother did that I try to practice is she hit people with the truth. If somebody was doing something wrong, she'd let them know it. If it had to be told in a loud, stern way, or in a softer way, they were going to hear what she perceived as being the truth. I have that same insight and it's helpful in breaking through the denial and isolation of relapse, where my gut tells me what I'm seeing is true.

When outreach workers go through a period of relapse, we don't kick them to the curb and say, "See ya. There are plenty of other people out there who can do the work." I help them to fight through the denial. I work with that person by being bluntly honest where most of the time it gets to the point where they admit where they're at. Maybe there are some deep personal issues that have surfaced they never dealt with. I give them both room and support to deal with them now.

People sometimes talk about the woman in me. That ability to empathize, to be a caretaker—qualities that are usually attributed to women I want to have part of me. The headstrong he-man, that is not me. I can cry, I can love, I can hug, I can talk about my weaknesses. Those attributes I learned from the women around me, starting with my mother. All human beings have empathy within them, but our culture drives it out of men. When I go to a meeting and it's volunteer work, most of the people in the room are likely to be women. But most meetings I attend where people are getting paid, the majority around the table are white men in suits.

Since I've been on the path of working for social change, the person who I can say I modeled myself after was my mother. Because on a deep, unconscious level, I was studying her. Her inner strength, her value on family, her wisdom in terms of dealing with everyday life problems, helping other people—all of those things that I possess today come from her.

My mother had traits I would like to say I have: the ability to reach people on a very human level, with an agenda that is not only a humanistic one, meaning to the betterment of people, but also an agenda that wasn't hidden, it was right out there. She was always a willing listener to other people's problems. She was always willing to invite someone over to eat if they didn't have something to eat. During the New Bedford riots, my mother was one of the women who cooked to make sure people had food when they were out there. What I'm trying to do and what's going to be my legacy is also my mother's legacy.

Being a grandfather is bittersweet for me. I have this great joy seeing how life goes through stages, and the natural order of things is you get to see grandchildren one day. I didn't think I would ever see that. My purest happiness comes from looking at them and knowing that's part of me that's still going to be here, and seeing that light in their eyes that hasn't been snuffed out yet. When I see how outgoing, self-confident, and how they want to learn, that to me is as a child should be. Then I think about the conditions under which they're going to have to live.

My feelings relating to the human condition have become, in a qualitative way, so fine-tuned that it affects me in both a negative and a positive way. The positive is I understand the value of the work I do and my part on the front lines in the struggle for humanity, for humans to reach another level of how we interact with one another. But having that understanding, the price I pay is having a lot of anguish—call it *empathy disorder*. When I look at the pain and suffering going on right now, it seems unbearable sometimes.

One Christmas Eve Shanté's mother was out walking her dog. Two police officers picked her up on an old warrant and took her in. Her boyfriend brought all her medicines to the jail—her psychiatric drugs plus the protease inhibitor. That Christmas morning I had just sat down and opened gifts with my daughter and Shelly, and I got a call—Maria said she's not being given any of her medicines. They also had her sleeping out in the hallway, which made her susceptible to colds and pneumonia, on top of her anxieties and depression. I couldn't enjoy the holiday knowing her situation and that there's other people in the same circumstances. I cried and got angry about it. I had to go through calling her doctor, calling my state senator, and staying on it for three days until she started getting her medicines.

Now if she was a diabetic, they probably would have given her her insulin. But because she's an addict and, in their terms, a fuckin' Black bitch junkie, she was denied her medication. If you don't take the protease inhibitor three times a day every eight hours, the virus can learn how to work around it. There's no guarantee that the next protease inhibitor will work on you. You're affecting not only her life, but also the community because she could, because of her situation, create a more resilient strain of the virus.

When someone tells me that I'm burned out, I'm too close to the issue when it comes to trying to get someone into a drug treatment program or getting a person their medicine, and you need to take time for yourself, my question is, how? There's a lot of pain out there and I have a lot of love in here. Che Guevera said, "Revolutionaries are guided by great feelings of love." I can empathize with people because I come from great suffering. A healthy, developed empathy for people will keep you on course, make sure you're doing things for the right reason, help you to make tough decisions, motivate you when you're tired and feel like you can't do any more.

Little things that happen that I'm effective at, like getting someone into a treatment program, help to massage me, help me to feel good, because they are situations where you can make an immediate difference. To change a policy is much harder. When I see how government policies and the economy are working hand in hand to create a large underclass, *POW* and *MIA* take on new meanings for me: *Poor Out of Work* and *Missing in America*—because we are in a full-fledged war.

When I look at the enormity of the issues, I have to find the balance and figure out what this one individual can do to make a difference. Look at the scope of things and put it in perspective: I'm just one person in a little city in a little state, in a bigger country, in a bigger world. We are all doing what I call God's work in our own way in our own little corners. Sometimes we can have an impact on a life, or sometimes we can have an impact on a city, a state, a country. There are people in Guatemala, South Africa, all over the world, who are trying to do some good. Some of them are probably where I'm at right now, empathy disorder, and thinking about it in the same way I do—that it's a good thing, not a bad thing. The worst thing to have is not empathy disorder, but apathy disorder.

My perception of AIDS as a part of the human condition is that there are some positives around it. One of the positives is it puts people in a position where we have to work together, because that's the only way we're going to be able to stop the virus from doing all that it's doing to me and to humankind. I believe when we as human beings look back at history and look at the time AIDS hit this planet and did all it did, some of the positive stories are not just going to be how people overcame and lived with the virus and how ordinary people did extraordinary things; the other story of AIDS is how it brought people together, different groups of people that up to then hadn't seen their commonality.

22

Facing the Reality of My Mortality

My experience living with the virus has been different in a lot of ways from those of many people. When I found out I had AIDS, my family all came and stood by me. From the day I knew, they knew. I didn't hold onto the secret as some people do where the secret becomes such a fear and burden that it's bigger than life. I never experienced what many people with the virus have experienced, where you're ostracized even by family members. My nieces can't wait for Uncle Gerald to hold their baby.

Halloween Day is my anniversary. It always brings up deep emotions, survivor's guilt being one. I think that most people go through life in a denial of death; most have that luxury where they don't think about it daily. But living with AIDS has put me in a position where I've had to deal with my mortality on a nose-to-nose, upfront-and-personal basis. Every day I'm steadily wrestling with that issue—both in my own life and in terms of people around me.

In the earlier part of the struggle, I would bounce between denial and complete fear. There was no real middle ground. Back in the beginning, I didn't think about it every day, especially the first five years when I was still active in my addiction. I spent more time thinking about not feeling. I didn't deal with my mortality where I thought about what it would be like to be sick, to go through one of those crises people with the virus go through.

When I got sick from one infection or another, hepatitis this or mono this, I was terrified because they originally told me I had a year or so to live. I remember the process of beginning to get sick with an opportunistic infection, pneumocystic pneumonia, and then getting real sick and being in the hospital with a high temperature they couldn't get down and all the fear that came along with that. When I finally left the hospital, I walked away with a sense of enlightenment, a feeling of accomplishment from going through this frightful experience. Up to that point, my perception was that the virus was not part of me, but something foreign that had invaded my body that I wanted to get out of me. But once I accepted the virus—like my addiction—was part of the total sum of who I was and what my life experience was, I found a kind of peace.

When my infectious disease doctor first spoke to me about the protease inhibitors, he compared them to a diabetic on insulin—this is how much faith he had put in them and what they could do for people with the virus. But I had got to this point where I had accepted the virus, accepted the fact I was not going to live a normal life in terms of my life span, and that death probably wasn't going to be a pretty sight. I don't think any death is, but the vision I've always had of the virus and what it does to the people over a period of time until they die: it's like taking a straw man and pulling him apart one straw at a time until there's nothing left.

I had a fear that if I bought into the hope about what the protease inhibitors were capable of doing, I would disrupt that place of acceptance I had found, especially if they didn't prove to be as successful as my doctor thought they would be. So I never allowed myself to totally buy into them. That ended up being a good thing for me, because after a year or so of taking protease inhibitors, the doctors found out my body was resistant to them. I had to go back to the old family of AIDS drugs, the AZT group. I got on a regimen of AZT, 3TC, and a new drug at that time called A*bacavir*.

The medicines are doing a job that is beneficial for my long-term survival. But every day I'm sick in terms of nausea, stomach pains, body aches, temperatures every now and then, and feeling lethargic and tired. There may be some breaks along the way where for several hours I feel pretty good and I'm not thinking about how I'm feeling physically. But there's a constant struggle of getting out of bed every morning, taking my medicines, making myself eat, because I have to take my pills with food, and then struggling to go to work.

I moved my office to my house to make it easier for me to work and take naps when I felt tired. But it was not that helpful. I canceled more meetings in one year than in my first ten years with Treatment on Demand. Some of it is not because I'm in a real physical crisis, but it's every day feeling the same way of tired, lethargic, weak, and nauseated, and it wears on you on a physical, emotional, and mental level.

Sometimes I can push the virus and what it's doing to me out of my mind and focus on my work. When I go to meetings outside of the house, people look at me and sometimes say, "You look good." Because I'm at the meeting and participating, their subjective view is that Gerald's doing good. But if you're Shelly, who sits with me and goes through it with me, she knows how much energy it takes for me to get to that place.

There's no getting used to waking up every day knowing your day's going to be miserable because of how you're feeling physically, which then affects you emotionally, which then affects you mentally. I sometimes feel like a dog chasing his tail. The cycle gets more intense, more difficult as I go along. Sometimes I get frustrated enough that I just want to throw up my hands and quit. I cannot picture being able to continue without having this compass that's pointing me in this direction where I'm saying to myself, "Your purpose is this and this is what you need to do" and then having the support to follow through on that.

It helps me to understand what I'm fighting for, to understand there are external forces that put people in this position where they have to experience so much pain and hardship in their lives. That understanding is what pushes me, that's what carries me when I'm doing work I don't really have the strength to do.

Sometimes I wholeheartedly believe in the work that I'm doing, that we human beings on this planet need to take responsibility to change things, to struggle against every kind of oppression. Then there's other times I wonder if I'm struggling with my own demons and this is how I deal with it—that I'm trying to right the wrongs I've done. Sometimes I'm clear that's not what it is, and sometimes I'm not so clear. Probably it's some of both. Sometimes it's more of one and less of the other.

Dealing with this *tick-tick-tick-tick* I hear in my head, I wonder how much time I've got left and how long I'm going to be able to do this work. It's a wonder I always live with. Sometimes it pushes me to do more than I had in the past or to take on more issues than I probably should. One of the lessons this disease has taught me, and it's always teaching me lessons, is I need to have more of a balance.

When my oldest daughter, Nsenga, was in nursing school, she had an assignment to talk to someone who was dealing with a chronic or terminal illness. At the end of her phone interview with me, I told her I felt the virus was a gift. She got quiet. I said, "What's the matter?" She replied, "I don't understand how you can say that. My father probably won't be here to see my kids grow up. Why would you say that?" She seemed perplexed, but I could also hear an edge of anger in her voice. I explained to her I saw it as a gift because it put passion in my life. "If someone came to you and said, 'I give you a gift and it's a gift of passion, which means that everything you do in life you will do to the best of your ability, you will always be in the moment. If you were cooking a meal, you would cook the best meal you could cook. If you were in school studying, you would study to the best of your ability. If you were listening to jazz, you would be in that moment and love the notes you were hearing. You would just really soak life in.' If someone could offer you that gift, would you take it?" She answered, "Yeah, of course I would." I said, "Well, that's sort of what the virus has done for me."

But it's not a gift you go out and seek. Although I still believe it has helped me in many ways, I don't put the same value on that gift as I did back then. When I talk about it being a gift, that gift should be given in other ways, not by getting a life-threatening disease. That was me the martyr talking at that time. I don't feel so much like a martyr today. It's because I love myself more today than I did then.

There's nothing much I can do about the situation, so I have to take what I've got and make it into a positive. One of my strong attributes is that I've been able to take a negative and see it as a positive. No experience is all negative if you learn from it. I believe the down periods in our lives are times when we're supposed to learn our most profound lessons in life. When I look at it in that sense, I say that when I come through this, I'm going to be an even stronger person with a much greater understanding.

You can try and be in denial about it, but the medicines are a constant reminder of what you're dealing with. You know this handful of pills that you're taking, like anything, there's positive and negative with them. You know it's doing some damage along with the good. In this instant gratification society we live in, when you take a medicine, you like to see a quick response: you get a headache, you take an aspirin and the headache goes away. Even when it came to the illegal drugs: you're feeling depressed, you take the drug, the depression goes away. You take the AIDS drugs, but you don't know what they're doing to your system in terms of being effective or not.

I know other people who are long-term survivors, who are dealing with this disease like I am, who talk about the frustration of taking their pills every day and the frustration of feeling sick every day. I've seen people who couldn't do it, won't do it, who've said, "I'm not taking any more pills. Life's going to take its course with me." I can see why people give up, because every day is a constant battle. People give up because of the frustration of taking these medicines and not seeing any short-term and, in many cases, long-term change.

Every three months or so I get blood work to test the viral load and find out is my body, along with the medicines, winning the struggle or not. Most of the time I come away feeling numb. Sometimes it's good news, which means that nothing has changed and the overall long-term prognosis is the same. Shelly is more likely to focus on the positive aspects of what we hear from the doctor than I am.

Most nights when I'm taking out my medicine bag, setting all the pill bottles in front of me, then putting the pills into the daily pill container, it's a major let-down for me. Sometimes I try to get into a place where I'm not even focusing on what I'm doing and trying to act like it ain't nothing. Other times that evening ritual is so frustrating that to get through it, I could be yelling and throwing the pills in the bag; it definitely changes the mood of the house at that moment.

I learned the importance of being compliant early on in the process of taking these AIDS drugs. When I first started taking them, no one explained to me the importance of not missing doses. I was missing doses, pills I was supposed to take three times a day I would sometimes take twice a day. Because my compliance at that point was probably around seventy, eighty percent, the virus mutated around them and those drugs which would have probably worked in me longer didn't work anymore.

Again, I have this fear about how am I going to get through this. When that question comes up, I say you've been through this before, you can go through it again. I also have a lot of resources in terms of friends I can depend on, including friends who are in the business of dealing with people who are addicts. For me, it's invaluable to have someone around me who can empathize with me but yet not be so caught up into it where it beats them down. They have the strength to say, "Hey, you gotta do this, hey, you gotta take this test. Yes, I know the test is invasive. Yes, I know it's painful. But I'll be there with you."

Because of the virus itself and/or the heavy-duty medicines I take, my common bile duct was damaged. Dealing with a lot of stomach pain brought up the issue of taking pain medicines and how that related to my addiction. I knew this was something I was going to have to deal with at some point because of this disease and how it attacks you.

Because I'm a recovering addict, the question I always wrestle with when I'm taking pain medication is, am I taking it because I want to feel good or because I want to feel better? *Feel good*, meaning do I want a buzz? *Feel better*, do I want to take away my pain? I think it's been both, and there are times it's been either one or the other. Thinking about it brings up a lot of anxieties. That and the fact that being on such a heavy dose of these pain medicines, at some level, has incapacitated me, where sometimes I have been doing little or no work.

In a lot of ways, it brings me back to that period where I was dependent on drugs. The fear of not being able to get it because the doctor might think you don't need it anymore, a sense of panic, to being locked up and those people who lock you up, for one reason or another, don't get you the medication. Just to be dependent in that way makes me feel almost like a victim. This is the issue I talk about with my doctors all the time, in terms of understanding why I'm on this medication and when am I going to get off it.

There have been times when we were talking about a medicine when the doctor said, "If and when you decide to get off this medicine—" I'm not sure what that means and I'm almost afraid to ask. I'm not sure if she thinks this will never be resolved in terms of the pain or if she thinks that for some reason it's not worth going through the pain and the process of getting off the medicine. It almost gives me a false sense of, well, you don't need to get off it, so that's not the issue. It's very confusing to me at times; it's also very terrifying on some levels. Sometimes I feel like just rolling up my sleeves and saying, "Let's get this over with." That is the impatient part of me, the part of me that, when I think something is inevitable, I just want to get it over with.

That mentality has gotten me into trouble in the past. When I tried one time to get off a high dose of methadone in a two-week period, I went through a lot of pain and cried to get back on it. Because of the rules of the program, I had to wait a month. So I struggle to maintain the thought process, "You had to be on it, now it's time to get off it. Let's take the right steps so it doesn't set you up to do the wrong thing."

I think about a friend, a recovering addict living with the virus, a community leader in Boston, who just before he died, was active again in his drug use. I wonder where he was at. Was he in the same place I'm at right now? Was he on pain medicine? Could he not get off it? Did he rush the process of getting off it? Did his doctors just cut him off of the pain medicines, making him think that his only option was to go to the street? Did he not have a strong, intimate support system around him? Did he lose his sense of purpose in life?

23

This Path I Took

When I reflect on my life and look at the changes I have gone through, it seems the end of each decade was a significant time for me in my personal development. I don't believe in fate in the sense that things are written to happen and they're going to follow that predestined pattern. When I look back at 1959, '69, '79, '89, and '99 as being transitional years, I think there's some irony, coincidence there—maybe the pattern is even forced. I also believe there's an ebb and flow to everything that happens in life in terms of nature, our own bodies, our lives, what happens in society. I even look at organizing in that way; sometimes it seems like things are exciting, you're getting ready to make a breakthrough, and then there's times when things are dull and quiet and almost at a standstill, like a winter.

In 1959, I began delivering papers on Hawthorn Street. I saw the inequality between that neighborhood and Purchase Street where I lived and tried to make sense of it.

Going into the armed forces in 1969 opened my eyes. I remember the bus trip down South during basic training, getting off on some back road and seeing the fields and the impoverished Black folks living alongside of them. I saw some of the world and I came to see my place in it differently. Many people who I grew up with never left the city. Some of them, the farthest they'd been was Boston, maybe New York. Living in different places, experiencing different cultures and subcultures broadens your understanding about yourself, because you have to come out of your comfort zone.

Going to Germany and seeing the racism over there, seeing how American companies had set up shop over there, I understood capitalism in a much broader, cleaner way. Meeting the ex-Panthers over there and being educated by them and building friendships with people who were from bigger cities and experiencing vicariously, through their lives, what they experienced—all of those encounters made me a much more informed, educated person.

I went to prison in 1979. To be in the belly of that pig, locked in that little cage and treated like an animal on some levels helped me to better understand the role that the criminal justice system plays in this country. It also forced me to think about some of the issues I had.

But that year in prison also pointed out that being locked up doesn't do anything for an individual in terms of helping them to deal with their issues, what put them there in the first place. Even though I was clearer than I ever had been about my addiction, I continued on getting high. There was nothing to replace it. So I ended up going back to it. I got my GED while I was in there, which shows that if things were available, I would have reached out. When people talk about prisons being just warehouses, I've experienced it.

I know what it's like to sit in there all day long, the thoughts that go through your mind, how you have to depend on your spirit to get through that. The Panthers used to say, "They can lock up your body but they can't lock up your soul." Depending on that spirit which developed during that year is something I've drawn on a lot since I left prison. Even now, when I'm having rough times in terms of dealing with my physical limitations because of disease, I have to say, "Yes, this is all true, but you're still alive. You still have a spirit and you can still transcend the situation that you're in."

In 1989, I co-founded Treatment on Demand. I was coming from a place where I was at an all-time low in my life physically, mentally, spiritually, relationship-wise. In most of the Eighties, I was caught in my addiction and finding out I was positive with the virus, chasing the dope all over and putting my life and other people's lives on the line, being homeless and not being with my family on any real level. To come to a place where I found some clarity about my life, come to a place where I could redefine who I was, come to a place where I rejoined the community, and come to a place where I began to see a purpose in my life and everything that I had experienced—it was like a rebirth. Getting involved with community work and then founding Treatment on Demand was the birthing process. Seeing myself as someone who could be a leader was an important part of who I am right now.

In 1999, I had my crisis of faith. Because of the physical, emotional, and spiritual issues I was facing, I had to pull back in some areas. I even questioned my capacity and creativity to do my work. Seeing me sick, weak, and tired all the time and the emotional toll that takes, people sometimes say, "If I was in that situation, I don't know if I could do it." I'm able to survive because I realize I'm not just a physical being, I'm also a mental being, I'm a spiritual being. Those are the parts of my life I can have some control over and not allow the illness to beat me down. Not that it hasn't beat me down, but it hasn't kept me down, because I have been able to pick myself back up.

I've learned how to make the best out of a situation. No matter how bleak it seems, I've been able to overcome it. According to the Buddhist way of thinking, every situation you experience—and they're talking specifically of the crises that happen in your life, be it an ending of a relationship, a death of a loved one, illness, poverty, all of those troubles that you face—you can grow from and the next thing that comes your way, you will be that much more prepared to deal with it.

There's also irony in the Treatment on Demand community center being on the same block where Susan and I opened up the record shop and, in front of that store, made the decision to get involved with the drug trade, with the naïve idea that we would sell drugs for a short time and pump that money into the legal business. Twenty-five years later I stood in front of the building that would become our community center and thought about how being on that same block was for me coming full circle in a healthy way.

Was I meant to take this path I took? My drinking early on was no different than most people in terms of how they end up using. Going through my addiction, the time I was snorting and the time I was shooting, I was still in the Superfly syndrome, where I thought that was where my life was supposed to be. When I got hooked to the level I did, I thought I was going beat it. I thought I was going to walk away from the addiction and get back into dealing, and that's where I was going to make a change, somehow, with the money.

It wasn't until I got the virus and got real sick that I started to make a change in terms of going back to my roots. My roots are in helping people. Reverend Chavier's analysis of who I was isn't much different than who I am today. The drug abuse and AIDS pandemics catapulted me into doing bigger things and I'm reaching people on a larger scale, because I am working in an organization I helped to found and I'm a public figure.

I believe that unless I went through all the different periods in my life, but specifically the period where the quality of my life was at its lowest, I wouldn't have the understanding I can bring to my work now. I wish I didn't have a disease that is not going to allow me to go naturally, so to speak. I wish I didn't have to deal with this disease on a daily basis. The fact that I do makes me more empathetic toward people, makes me realize even more than I probably would have that I am a mortal creature and not here forever. My goals might be up there among the stars, but living with AIDS keeps me firmly planted on the ground.

Living with the AIDS virus, I have to stay in reality and that's what gives me my passion for life, that's what makes me say, "Hey, today's today, you don't know about tomorrow. So you've got to do the best you can on everything you do, because you might not have a chance to do it again." That awareness keeps me grounded and does not allow for me to spend too much time in the past reminiscing. I'm trying to just live in the moment and deal with issues that are relevant today.

The work that I do now encompasses everything I've done in the past. Everything that happened to me in the past makes me successful at what I do, from being involved with church, from being a paper boy—I used to deliver papers and was good at that, used to get it done and get the big tips—to being in the Army and getting to understand the global picture, to opening up the businesses, to being a drug dealer—all of that helped create what I am and helped me to become an organizer. Because what is an organizer? An organizer is someone who has vision, can have five things working at the same time at different levels, and understands how they all impact on each other.

There is some past that has a future for me I have to deal with. Though I might have made a choice years ago based on the negative influences around me, I still made the choice. I can say it was because I come from a social class which has been disenfranchised, where I did not see the opportunities. I blame the system that I live in to a degree. I take responsibility for my recovery from that.

I take responsibility for redefining who I am in spite of all that. I also have to take responsibility for some of the deeds I did back then. The fact that I have five children with three women; I am a father, but being a parent is a different thing. The fact that I wasn't a parent to all of those children is something I will live with, that I will have to carry to my grave. There are some things you can't do anything about in terms of going back and changing, but you can try to deal with them the best you can today.

So I try to connect with my children now. I try to be the best parent for the daughter who lives with me and try to give her as many tools as I can to deal with being a poor Black woman in this society. I try to arm her to look at racism, classism, and sexism and say, "In spite of that, I can still be a positive to myself and to those around me." Even if other people look and see it, she won't be happy unless she sees that value in herself.

Part of me still wrestles with my baby brother's death. I have never got to a point where I totally accepted what my mother said about it not being my fault. Even if I did play a role in his death, I should be able to accept the fact that I was a child and it was an accident. I believe if I could come to terms with what happened, it would have a qualitative effect on how I feel about myself and how much I enjoy life and could learn from things that happen. I could say, well, that happened and learn from it as opposed to sometimes saying, that happened, you deserved it. It's an issue I hope I come to terms with some day before I make the transition over to the next world. I would hate to be on my deathbed and have that be the last thought running through my mind.

The fact that I've lived more than fifteen years with the virus and so many people have died before me, and I'm still here, still limping along doing this work, I believe in my heart was supposed to happen. I have doubts. My doubts usually revolve around my ability to get something done. I deal with my doubts by seeing the importance of the goal in mind. Once I understand the importance of getting it done, then I have to put the doubts aside and go by faith that it will happen. While I might not use the word *faith* a lot, I am definitely a person of faith. I have to be in terms of trying to be an effective leader within the context of living with a terminal disease and wondering from time to time whether I'm going to be around for this or that. I have to have faith sometimes just to get up in the morning and get through the day. That's something I got from my mother. She was a woman of faith.

There is part of me that wishes things could have been different, in the sense that the opportunities were there for me to become what I envisioned myself to become when I was a child. How can I say I don't regret being able to have all the resources and the support to become a veterinarian? But when I weigh that against the importance of the work I'm doing, the work that I'm part of, which is not so much just whether Gerald gets the resources he needs, but that human beings in general have what they need to become what they want to become, that's much more important to me than fulfilling my childhood dream to become a veterinarian.

Where I love animals, it's hard to say how much pleasure I would have gotten out of that. But in the larger scheme of things, I believe the work I'm doing as a human being, trying to help all human beings, is the most important thing anybody can do.

I believe to my core I was meant to do this kind of work. It's not so much that I think I'm good at what I do, but it's more I'm comfortable doing what I do. I love what I do. I can be happy that I am able to move things along, happy that I'm able to reach some people in a profound way where they make changes, but the negative side, the chain around my neck is knowing that this work wouldn't be necessary if people weren't suffering.

There's a contradiction there, but I guess I can live with that because I'm not in it for self-gain. What's your agenda? What are you trying to gain and to what expense and to whose expense? I am doing what I think is right to help me and to help other people like me. And people like me are every human being that walks the earth, no matter what color or race, where they come from, young or old—we're all connected.

Coming up in the church and having a spiritual base, I helped create an organization that values all people. No one that's living and breathing should be written off. That's a tough position to take, when you look at some of the things people have done. Even when I read a news story and am appalled, I always try to pull myself back and say, "This is a human being. At some level, at some point, at some time, something happened to this person which created an illness in them or, as someone put it, some kind of *dis-ease* in that person, and when people have *dis-ease*, they tend to act out in some way." If people wrote me off because of my *dis-ease*, based on my life experiences, they were wrong, because I feel that I am not that troublemaker, nigger, junkie, scum-of-the-earth person.

So what I do is for me. I know when I'm sitting down talking to some young person and trying to reach them, in some ways I'm trying to talk to that young person that was me at one time. When I'm sitting there talking to somebody in a hospital bed that's having a particularly rough time living with the virus, I'm talking to me. I know that's what's going on. That's the selfish part I realize is there that I have no guilt about. I think it's a natural part of the recovery process and to deny it is not a good thing.

What I have to deal with is how do I best use my life experience and my awareness and whatever talents were given to me. That's what I need to focus on until the day I die. If I am able to do this work better, it is because I'm getting better at loving myself and knowing who I am.

I like to say I'm a truth-seeker and a truth-sharer, and the truth I share is my own life experience and the critical thinking that has come out of it. If you cut me down to the essence of who I am and what I'm about, that's what it is. And if that's what I truly am, it makes it easy for me not to be seduced by drugs or public recognition.

I see myself as a person who is trying to be part of something in the overall struggle for human rights. I don't see myself as being special, on a pedestal. As long as I believe that, and I do to my core, then that becomes like armor to all of those pitfalls other people have succumbed to. I just continue on with my compass pointed north. I'm just going to do what I think I was sent here to do.

Notes

Foreword

[1] Julia Alvarez, *In the Time of Butterflies* (Chapel Hill, NC: Algonquin Books, 1994), p. 313.

[2] Bertrand Russell, "The Future of Mankind," in his *Unpopular Essays* (New York: Simon and Schuster, 1950), p. 36.

[3] Jim Yong Kim, Joyce V. Millen, Alec Irwin, and John Gershman, eds., *Dying for Growth: Global Inequality and the Health of the Poor* (Monroe, ME: Common Courage Press, 2000).

[4] James Olney, *Metaphors of Self: The Meaning of Autobiography* (Princeton, NJ: Princeton University Press, 1972), p. viii.

[5] Edward W. Said, *Culture and Imperialism* (New York: Vintage Books, 1994)., p. 336.

[6] Paulo Freire, *Pedagogy of the Oppressed*, trans. Myra Bergman Ramos (New York, NY: Continuum Publishing, 1999), p. 38.

4/Liberated Territory

[7] *Jag* (*jagacida*) is a staple Cape Verdean dish of rice and beans.

[8] In response to two police raids that occurred in January-February 1968 in the San Francisco Bay area, Huey Newton, Minister of Defense of the Black Panther Party, issued the directive to which Gerald refers (titled "Executive Mandate No. 3") on March 1, 1968—that is, before the 1969-70 nationwide campaign of state repression against the Panther Party (E-mails to Robert French from Professor Jama Lazerow, Professor of History, Wheelock College, March 22, 2004 and April 1, 2004).

[9] The United Front in New Bedford was related to, and sometimes called, the Black United Front, organized in Boston in early 1968 through the efforts of Stokely Carmichael (E-mail to French from Lazerow, March 22, 2004).

[10] Twenty-one people were arrested in the July 31, 1970 raid, although the press put the number at twenty. Charges against four were quickly dropped. Gerald's return to New Bedford in October 1970 after being discharged from the Army coincided with a Bristol County Grand Jury's indictment of ten of the defendants. The new District Attorney, however, dropped the principal charges (of conspiracy to commit anarchy, etc.) against all just before the March 29, 1971 trial date. Only one was convicted; his six months' sentence for unlawful possession of a firearm was later suspended. A leaflet (recently released by the FBI) announcing a demonstration at the Superior Court the morning of the trial is headed "Free the New Bedford 20"—the most common tag used to refer to the defendants (E-mails to French from Lazerow, March 23, 2004 and June 4, 2004).

17/Stayin' Alive

[11] In his support of needle exchange, Gerald noted that among those who inject drugs, African Americans and Latino/as are much more likely to contract HIV/ AIDS than whites because of pervasive racist bias in police searches, arrest, prosecution, and imprisonment. In an Op-Ed piece, he writes, "According to FBI findings, black addicts are arrested at a rate four times higher than white addicts. Therefore, with the increased threat of arrest, black addicts are less likely to carry their own needles and more likely to share needles. The result of the targeting of blacks for drug use, coupled with the illegality of needle possession, has been the disproportionate spread of AIDS in the black community' (Gerald S. Ribeiro, "AIDS doesn't discriminate; why do we?" *The Standard-Times* (New Bedford, Massachusetts), March 29, 1999).

[12] While focused on reducing the individual and social harms related to drug use, especially the risk of HIV infection, Gerald did not have a problem with assigning a positive value to helping addicts to become drug free, even if it was a distant goal. He took issue with the perspective that harm reduction should be neutral regarding long-term desired outcomes for addicts. In staking out his position, he found support in the very heart of harm reduction theory—i.e., that harm reduction programs measure success on the basis of individual and community quality of life rather than levels of drug use. Drawing from his own experience as a

cocaine and heroin addict, he asked rhetorically, what quality of life does someone enjoy when their day-to-day existence revolves around getting high, being high, living in poverty, and engaging in criminal activity to obtain drugs? He also noted that, inasmuch as many addicts commit property and violent crimes to get drugs, the quality of life in a community is invariably compromised by drug addiction among its members.

18/About Political Capital and Me

[13] Ivory Perry (1930-1989) was a grassroots activist in St. Louis in the struggle for civil rights and social change. His life and work are documented in George Lipsitz, *A Life in the Struggle: Ivory Perry and the Culture of Opposition*, rev. ed. (Philadelphia: Temple University Press, 1995). Gerald said, "Like Ivory Perry, I received my education through living life. His story helped me not only politically, but on a personal level. He had a couple of nervous breakdowns on account of the stress of the work—which I could relate to having experienced burnout. While many American Black heroes like Malcolm X and George Jackson seem larger than life, Ivory Perry was more human, more accessible to me, and more realistic for me to aspire to. His example made it seem possible for me to tell my own story."

[14] In his work and his personal life, Gerald often spoke about the importance of keeping a sense of direction, purpose, and proportion. A recurrent metaphor in the interviews for this book is his inner compass to maintain a northward direction—surely alluding to the northward flight of escaped slaves in their quest for freedom. During the 1800s, New Bedford, Massachusetts had many Underground Railroad "stations" for hiding and aiding fugitive slaves. Known as a safe haven for runaways, New Bedford's African American population grew to nearly 700 in 1850. One of the most prominent anti-slavery leaders, Frederick Douglass, lived his first years as a free man in New Bedford.

978-0-595-37824-1
0-595-37824-2